D1601585

THE
MEANING
AND MYSTERY
OF MAN

THE
MEANING
AND MYSTERY
OF MAN

THE ROLE AND RESPONSIBILITY OF THE CHRISTIAN MAN:
A BIBLICAL STUDY OF ADAM, ST. JOSEPH AND JESUS CHRIST

DEVIN SCHADT

TAN Books
Gastonia, North Carolina

Excerpts from the English translation of the *Catechism of the Catholic Church*, Second Edition, ©1994, 1997, 2000 by Libreria Editrice Vaticana, United States Catholic Conference, Washington, D.C. All rights reserved.

Unless otherwise noted, Scripture quotations are from the Douay-Rheims version of Sacred Scripture. Copyright 1914 by John Murphy Company

Cover Design: Devin Schadt

ISBN: 978-1-5051-2251-0
Kindle ISBN: 978-1-5051-2252-7
ePUB ISBN: 978-1-5051-2253-4

Published in the United States by
TAN Books
PO Box 269
Gastonia, NC 28053
www.TANBooks.com

Licensed from
Stewardship: A Mission of Faith
11 BlackHawk Lane
Elizabethtown, PA 17022
StewardshipMission.org

Printed in the United States

CONTENTS

A Search for the Divine Vision of Man

G od has imparted men with the noble task to establish peace, sometimes with the sword; to unite peoples by proclaiming the truth, a truth that often divides; and to, in the name of God, lead their families, which demands that they learn to follow Christ.

As of late, though, it appears that the true Christian man has become a byword, and his glory has all but faded. He is plagued by a haunting, hidden shame for his desire to exercise his God-given power and authority for the purpose of following Christ's mandate to save souls.

This is not accidental. The devil is acutely aware that the conversion of the world depends on a thriving, faithful, Church militant; that an uncompromising, life-giving Church is dependent upon faithful, godly families who pursue holiness and love sacrificially; and that families such as these are dependent upon the husband, the father, to lead his family to salvation in Jesus Christ. If that man is shamed into suppressing his authority and power, the divine project to save mankind is gravely compromised.

If a man is married, has children, and is serious about his responsibility to Christ and his family, he senses that he is being summoned to spiritual combat, to be the spiritual leader of his family. He responds to his heavenly Commander's voice, the battle drum of divine inspiration, the horn beckoning him to the front lines of what could be one of the greatest spiritual battles of all ages.

Yet, when he arrives at the field of decision, scrambling into formation with others like himself, he looks for those commanders who have the answers to his identity, his destiny, his mission, and his vocation. What is his location in the battle? What position should he take? What is his role and his responsibility? Who answers to him, and to whom does he answer?

It is for lack of vision that the people perish,[1] and for lack of true shepherds that the flock flees and falls.[2] The world continually demands that men, in the name of equality and diversity, apologize for their masculinity and that they never forget their

---

1   See Prv 29:18.
2   See Zec 13:7.

former misuse of that power, which is often considered a phenomenon of pancultural domination of women.

When a man apologizes, he attempts to right the wrong he has inflicted. Yet, if he denies who he is, he cannot repent of his wrongdoing. The world incessantly demands that men, particularly Christian husbands and fathers, apologize for the misuse of their fatherly authority by denying or suppressing the very identity and authority that enables them to right the wrong.

The answer to upholding women is not to spiritually neuter or obliterate male headship, but rather to understand it for what it actually is, to proclaim its glorious, biblical, theological vision, and to live it fully.

To adapt a well-known statement of the Venerable Archbishop Fulton Sheen for our use: There exist a multitude of people who hate patriarchal authority and male headship for what they think it is; and yet very few who despise it for what it truly is. This misrepresentation is the chief reason for this work.

What is male headship actually? What is patriarchal authority as God intended it to be? Can we, in the modern age, dare to believe, proclaim, and embody such ideas?

This book is not a practical, how-to, step-by-step, self-help book about being an involved dad or an attentive, nice husband. It doesn't contain any inspirational personal stories. This piece will not reflect upon the woman's role, her genius, or her contribution to the Church, to marriage, and to the family. Nor will this work focus on the suppression of women's rights and how this evil ought to be rectified. In this regard, the Church offers many valuable resources.[3]

This book is an attempt to mine the riches of Sacred Scripture and the traditional thought that is continually expressed by the Church for the purpose of proposing a theological, perhaps mystical, vision of man that is biblical, practical, and hopefully inspirational.

God, in His generosity, has packed Sacred Scripture with many insights particular to the nature, essence, role, and responsibility of man. As many of these truths were common sense, based on natural law, or embedded in the liturgy of the Church, there was no need for them to be formally defined. Yet, the cultural, sexual revolution that began in the 1960s has undermined, eclipsed, and potentially redefined the traditional understanding of man and his mission, robbing him of his unique spiritual influence.

In our age, the man who is husband, father, and head of his home, must be re-visited with a determination to define him, his

---

3   For example, see John Paul II, *Letter of John Paul II to Women* (1995); John Paul II, *Mulieris Dignitatem*. Hereafter *MD*.

role, and his responsibility in a theologically and scripturally accurate way.

What are the chief spiritual characteristics of the man that make him unique and complementary to the woman? Why did God create him in this way; and what constitutes his official station in life? Why is he essential to God's plan to save humanity?

To develop adequate responses to these questions, we will mine the sacred texts for the purpose of discovering the divinely intended meaning of man by returning to the original man, Adam, and typologically comparing him to the God-man, the New Adam, Jesus Christ.

Yet, located between these two men exists the "just man," St. Joseph, who in many ways is a fulfillment of the Old Adam, "the man of the Old Testament." At the same time, he is a typological precursor for his Son, Jesus Christ, the New Adam. St. Joseph, therefore, "is like to a man that is a householder, who bringeth forth out of his treasure new things and old" (Mt 13:52). Therefore, St. Joseph is an essential bridge between the original man and the God-man, who will aid us in our attempts to unveil a full vision of the mature man in Christ.

Unfortunately, the satanic agenda to destroy the Church by re-defining and undermining the mission of the *ecclesia domestica,* the family, is well underway and, perhaps, reaching its final stages.

There, however, exists one—the faithful husband and father—who has been entrusted with the task to hold fast at the helm and, by means of having the divine vision of his mission and office, navigate those entrusted to him to the shores of victory in Christ.

In the final analysis, the key to converting the nations is the renewal and strengthening of the Church, in numbers and faith; and the key to renewing the *ecclesia universalis*, the universal Church, is restoring the *ecclesia domestica*, the domestic church (the family), that it may reflect the image of the Trinity; and the key to restoring the family to this noble identity is the revitalization of marriage; and, to accomplish this, the man who is appointed by God to be the head of his house, the head of the family, must understand his meaning and mission and manifest the glory of God in his spiritual paternity.

Each section of this book will be comprised of detailed scriptural meditations that compare the Old Adam and the New Adam by linking them with St. Joseph. With this in mind, the first section of this work, *A New Genesis,* demonstrates St. Joseph's vital position as this link between the original and the redeemed man, while also acclaiming his vital necessity in formulating a full vision of man.

Proceeding from this first section, the following four sections focus on a particular, fundamental aspect of man's role and responsibility. When these four aspects are combined, they will constitute an outline for a theological, scriptural, somewhat practical, inspirational vision of the meaning of man in God, and God in man. These four sections are: *The Guardian of the Garden: Defining Man's Position in God's Plan*; *Man's Role and Responsibility: The Hierarchy of Sacrificial Responsibility*; *A Husband's Headship: At the Service of Completing the Bride*; and *Patriarchal Authority: At the Service of Completing the Family*.

Lest it even need mentioning, the truths presented in this book will run contrary to the numerous false ideologies proposed by the world and the devil. The world will not receive this message. This work is a sign of contradiction to the world's false formulations of marriage, family, and humanism. Yet, this body of work contains the fundamental remedy to the disorders that have assaulted marriage, that have attempted to redefine the family, and that have undermined the authority of the Catholic Church and the Gospel of Jesus Christ.

May these meditations be a blessing to you in your search and desire to become the man God has created you to be.

St. Joseph, head of the Holy Family, ora pro nobis.

The Genesis creation accounts are divinely inspired, theological-mystical literature, which we will examine in detail in hope of clearly understanding man's role, responsibility, and meaning. We will not be referring to the divinely inspired creation accounts as a historical-scientific literary genre. By penetrating the Sacred Text, we endeavor to discover symbols and figures that aid us in unveiling the divine vision of the true man—a vision that has practical implications for our modern world.

CHAPTER 1

The New Genesis

Man: A Mystery unto Himself

My brother, you are a mystery unto yourself. You know yourself, and yet you know yourself not. You have lived your life, and yet your life to live remains. You have an unknown destiny that is dependent upon you knowing and embracing your identity. Yet, few know themselves because they know not the God who created them. Nor do they pursue the One who is already pursuing them.

Your life has been divinely designed and ordained to be a continual unfolding of the mystery of your identity, which if understood and embraced will lift you from the allurements of the world, magnetically drawing you into the adventure of receiving, and in a certain sense achieving, your God given destiny. To paraphrase St. Augustine, "God who created you without you will not save you without you."[4] God has given you your mission, which you must receive, but you, my brother, must fulfill that mission.[5]

Every man is afforded the opportunity and power to know himself, but to fully realize oneself is an arduous life-long work that demands the peeling back of those false veneers that mask the true self.

Man is allured and smitten by objects, creatures, and enticements in which he unsuccessfully attempts to find value, meaning, and his true self. If a man identifies himself with things that change, his identity changes with those things. He becomes unknown, incomprehensible to himself, a black hole of self-absorption that suffocates the flame of the mystery of himself, and a fragile flame that is intended to be fanned into a fire that sets the world ablaze.[6] To modify a modern phrase

---

4   "*The preparation of man* for the reception of grace is already a work of grace. This latter is needed to arouse and sustain our collaboration in justification through faith, and in sanctification through charity. God brings to completion in us what he has begun, 'since he who completes his work by cooperating with our will began by working so that we might will it' (St. Augustine, *De gratia et libero arbitrio*, 17; PL 44, 901)." St Augustine, *Sermo 169*, 13 (PL 38, 923); See also *CCC*, 2001.

5   "God's free initiative demands man's free response, for God has created man in his image by conferring on him, along with freedom, the power to know him and love him." *CCC*, 2002.

6   "Be who God meant you to be and you will set the world on fire." St. Catherine of Siena.

to fit our purposes: such men are "souled" out, that is, they have exchanged their souls for the fleeting trinkets that the superficial world offers.

There is great power in God's plan, and, if this plan is embraced, your life will be one of great power.

> For by his interior qualities he outstrips the whole sum of mere things. He plunges into the depths of reality whenever he enters into his own heart; God, Who probes the heart (1 Kgs 16:7, Jer 17:10) awaits him there; there he discerns his proper destiny beneath the eyes of God. (*Gaudium et Spes*, 14)

By delving deeply into the mines and chasms of self, man discovers his deficiencies and his incessant longing for the sufficient, his emptiness and his desire to be full, and his hope to love another and be loved by another.

By entering the caverns and labyrinths of self you will encounter a perplex riddle: those things to which you wish to attach yourself for the purpose of supplying yourself value and significance are the very things that you must detach from in hopes of obtaining eternal and significant value.

Indeed, by diving deeply into himself, man discovers the God who has dived deeply into him, and he encounters the God who awaits him in his soul. Your project, my brother, is to examine your life's foundation, the very reason of your personal existence, why you have been created, and for what and for whom you have been created. It is our task to encounter God within us—the God who calls us to ascend beyond worldly significance and become a revelation of His glory.

God has created you to be unique and unrepeatable, to be a manifestation and revelation of His divine presence to this breaking, if not broken, world.[7] You are to express the unique presence of the living God that dwells within you—a presence that manifests itself in a wholly unique way—to the world around you.

Yet, the man who derives meaning from things whose meanings change is compromised in his ability to reflect the unchanging God. If a man clings to a false identity, he suppresses the glory of God that is meant to be revealed through him.

You have a mission that is universal, yet uniquely personal. It is your task, through prayer, silence, and a listening heart, to wait on the Word to speak this mission into you—understanding

---

7 "For God and before God, the human being is always unique and unrepeatable, somebody thought of and chosen from eternity, someone called and identified by his own name." John Paul II, *Urbi et Orbi* (Christmas Day 1978).

that the Word has already spoken and has breathed and knit this Word into your soul.

The Word always speaks, but rarely does He find one who is inclined toward listening. There exist few men who are courageous enough to sacrifice the voices of this world for the purpose of making space for the Word. How can they know themselves, let alone claim to know the God who created them, if they refuse to silence themselves before the God who speaks in silence? Such a man's identity is all but lost and losing his identity he suffers the loss of his destiny.

Be not like them. If you attentively listen to the Word that has spoken and continually is speaking in your soul, you will be granted power to rise above the universe of objects and creatures toward your destiny—a partaking in the glory of God.

The Original Cause

Though God's presence dwells within you personally, it is never enough to examine yourself as a man in isolation from the universal man. To attain your destiny, it is imperative to examine the foundations of your identity; and to understand the ultimate mission and destiny of every man, you must examine the foundations, identity, and mission of the universal man, whose identity has fallen into obscurity and miscomprehension. Man knows little of himself for he knows little of what it means to be a man. Man knows little of himself for he knows little of God.

To know and realize your individual end, it is imperative to comprehend man's universal beginning.[8] To successfully press forward as men, it is necessary to return to the origins of man. Indeed, by returning to the first man, we will discover more fully the purpose and plan of every man.

Christ Himself, when interrogated by the Pharisees on the question of the legality of divorce, directed these Jewish leaders to ponder the plan from the beginning:

> And there came to him some Pharisees, testing him, and saying, "Is it lawful for a man to put away his wife for *any cause?*" But he answered and said to them, "Have you not read that the Creator, from the beginning, made them male and female, and said, *for this cause a man shall leave his father and mother, and cleave to his wife, and the two shall become one flesh?* Therefore, now they are no longer two but one flesh.

---

8   "So that the goal of this journey might be clear and consequently the way plainly indicated, the Synod was right to begin by considering in depth the original design of God for marriage and the family: it 'went back to the beginning,' in deference to the teaching of Christ" (cf. Mt 19:4–6). John Paul II, *Familiaris Consortio,*10. Hereafter *FC.*

What therefore God has joined together, let no man put asunder." They said to him, "Why then did Moses command to give a written notice of dismissal, and to put her away?" He said to them, "because Moses, by reason of the hardness of your heart, permitted you to put away your wives; but it was not so from the beginning." (Matthew 19:3–8, emphasis added)

This question of divorce is a question of masculine responsibility. The Jewish leaders, comprised of men, posed the perennial question: How do we men legally shirk our moral responsibility?

By cheating God of themselves, men cheat themselves of God, and, by giving God less of themselves, they receive less of God. The question is not as much about man and divorce, but rather the divorce within man himself. The Pharisee's question is telling in that it testifies to man's desire to *divorce masculinity from responsibility*; and, if man successfully divorces masculinity from responsibility, he separates himself from his God-given mission and identity.

Our Lord focuses on the intent of the Pharisees question: Can I divest myself of responsibility for the woman and the child she bears for *any cause*? Jesus' response begins with "for this cause." Rather than looking at negative causes that are used to excuse man from his responsibility for the woman, the child, and the family, Jesus asks us to examine the root cause of man's role and responsibility.

Christ directs us to return to the beginning and discover the original cause for marriage and to consequently discover the role and responsibility of each and every man. By returning to the first man, we will discover the universal purpose and plan of every man as God intended him to be, while also receiving counsel regarding our particular mission.[9]

However, the original man will not be sufficient for us to comprehend God's ultimate, fulfilled vision of man. Indeed, masculinity finds its fulfillment in spiritual paternity; that is, the pinnacle of manhood is only discovered in spiritual fatherhood.

Adam failed to protect the image and likeness of God that dwelled within himself and his wife and thus allowed the serpent to malign this likeness from them and their human descendants prior to Christ. Because of this, it is necessary to look to the example of another man who did not fail in being a spiritual father, who protected the image of God incarnate, and *the woman* who bore him to the world.

Just as we cannot discover the personal man without comprehending the universal man, so also we cannot understand

---

9   "Accordingly, the family must go back to the 'beginning' of God's creative act, if it is to attain self-knowledge and self-realization in accordance with the inner truth not only of what it is but also of what it does in history." *FC*, 17.

the universal Adam's beginning without comprehending the fulfillment of this Adam in the new beginning. We must not only return to the genesis of man, but also proceed to a *New Genesis* in which the original, universal man was fulfilled.

There exists a link between the last Adam and the eternal New Adam, between David and the Son of David, between God the Father and God the Son of the Father, and between the genesis of man and the revelation of the God-man.

St. Joseph the son of David,[10] the supposed father of the Son of David,[11] became a spiritual father to God the Son and is a typological fulfillment of the Old Adam, while also being a typological foreshadowing of the ultimate and eternal New Adam, Jesus Christ. Without producing a son biologically, St. Joseph became Jesus' father spiritually.[12]

---

10 See Mt 1:20.

11 "Jesus the son of Joseph of Nazareth." Jn 1:45; [And Mary, after finding Jesus in the temple after three days] "and seeing him, they wondered. And his mother said to him: Son, why hast thou done so to us? Behold thy father and I have sought thee sorrowing." Lk 2:48; "St. Augustine holds this point of view: 'To [Joseph] also was the command given to bestow the name on the Child, although the Child was not born of his seed . . . of Joseph's seed, when, while wondering how Mary became pregnant, he is told, "It is of the Holy Spirit." Nonetheless, paternal authority is not taken away from him, for he is commanded to name the Child. Finally, the Virgin Mary herself calls him father of Christ.'" Francis L. Filas, S.J., *Joseph and Jesus: A Theological Study of Their Relationship* (Milwaukee, Wisconsin, The Bruce Publishing Company, 1952, p 39. Hereafter *Joseph and Jesus: A Theological Study of Their Relationship*.

12 St. Bernadine of Siena, Doctor of the Church, said, "Who, I ask, will deny that while Joseph held Christ in his arms as a father and spoke to Him as a father.

By returning to the genesis of the original Adam and comparing it with the *New Genesis* of St. Joseph, we will begin to discover a fuller vision of the meaning of man in Jesus Christ. It is from this man, St. Joseph, and his relationship with Christ and Mary that we will begin to discover *the cause* and reason for the existence of man. Whereas Adam was the beginning of life's end, St. Joseph, always in union with Mary, is the new beginning of a never-ending life.[13] It is by following this man, St. Joseph, that you may experience a new beginning also.

The New Beginning

St. Matthew's Gospel begins with the words "the book of the *origin* of Jesus, the Son of David, the Son of Abraham" (Mt 1:1,emphasis

---

. . . He impressed ineffable joys upon him! O with what sweetness he hears the lisping Child call him father! With a love that transformed him, he was attracted to [Jesus], as to his dearest son presented him by the Holy Spirit in his virginal wife." And again, "This holy man had such towering dignity and glory that the Eternal Father most generously bestowed on him a likeness of His own primacy over His son incarnate." And according to Knabenbauer, citing Bellouvet, "Joseph is called the father of Jesus because he truly contributed to His origin; for according to the divine plan Jesus was to be born of a virgin wife. The continence of Joseph constituted his fatherhood as a cause in the moral order" *(Joseph and Jesus: A Theological Study of Their Relationship, p 143).*

13 "We see that at the beginning of the New Testament, as at the beginning of the Old, there is a married couple. But whereas Adam and Eve were the source of evil which was unleashed on the world, Joseph and Mary are the summit from which holiness spreads all over the earth. The Savior began the work of salvation by this holy virginal union." John Paul II, *Redemptoris Custos (Guardian of the Redeemer)*, 7. Hereafter *RC.*

added), and "now the *origin* of Christ was in this wise" (Mt 1:18, emphasis added). The word origin, used in both verses to describe the beginnings of Jesus, is the English rendering of the Greek noun *genesis*. By using the word *genesis*, Matthew is echoing the original creation account, connecting man's beginning in Adam to the new beginning of men in St. Joseph, "the father of Jesus."[14]

Later, in the first chapter of St. Matthew's Gospel,[15] we discover more convincing evidence of the Evangelist's intention to proclaim a "new beginning," a *New Genesis* in the marriage of Joseph and Mary.

> So all the generations, from Abraham to David, are fourteen generations. And from David to the transmigration of Babylon, are fourteen generations: and from the transmigration of Babylon to Christ are fourteen generations. Now the generation of Christ was in this wise. (Matthew 1:17–18)

Matthew relates that the history of God's people preceding Jesus Christ was comprised of three sets of fourteen generations. In other words, six sets of seven generations. Each of these six sets symbol-

---

14   "Jesus . . . being (as it was supposed) the son of Joseph." Lk 3:23.
15   See Mt 1:17.

ize the original genesis account consisting of six days of creation.[16]

The generation of Christ within the marriage of Mary and Joseph constitutes the seventh generation, a symbol of the seventh day in the Genesis creation account in which God covenants (oaths) Himself to mankind.

Though the original covenant was repeatedly broken by God's people throughout the six sets of seven generations, nevertheless God remains faithful to His people by establishing a New Covenant of eternal sonship in Jesus Christ. Thus, the seventh set of the seven generations symbolizes a completion in God's creation and redemption of His people as marked by the seventh day in the creation account.

It is very likely that St. Matthew is drawing a correlation between Adam and Eve, who were appointed to become a bridge between the generations occurring on the sixth day (that of the beasts) and the covenant made on the seventh day (that of divine sonship), and St. Joseph, a New Adam, and the Blessed Virgin Mary, the New Eve. This holy couple successfully bridges the six sets of generations of God's people to the seventh, final, and eternal generation of divine sonship won by Jesus Christ.

This concept of a new beginning, a new order of grace, a *New*

---

16 See Gn 1.

Genesis in the holy virginal couple of Mary and Joseph, also appears to be a key theme in the Gospel of St. Luke:

> Now in the sixth month the angel Gabriel was sent from God to a town of Galilee called Nazareth, to a virgin betrothed to a man named Joseph, of the house of David, and the virgin's name was Mary. (Luke 1:26–27)

It appears that St. Luke is intentionally, artistically, and, with rich symbolism, portraying the actual historical event of the Annunciation as an account of a new creation. The phrase "in the sixth month" echoes and typologically fulfills the creation account in Genesis wherein on the sixth day three things of tremendous import occur: first, the sinless, virgin Adam was created; second, it was from Adam that God formed the virgin woman and gave her being; and third, the couple entered into a covenant with God and one another.

The sixth month of Elizabeth's pregnancy symbolizes the sixth day of creation in which man is created with the animals, and yet he is also created for the seventh day. This seventh day of rest is the day in which God vowed Himself to man; and man, expressed by his rest in God, vowed himself to God.

Again, man moves from the sixth day, the day of the beast

(the mark of the base animal) to the seventh day, the day of divinization, the Day of the Lord.

The event of the Annunciation during the "sixth month" marks a pivotal transition, a turning point for fallen humanity that has repeatedly chosen to live as a base animal—bound by its fleshly passions and the seduction of sin—rather than as a transformed and divinized child of God.

In Mary's womb, during the sixth month of her cousin Elizabeth's pregnancy, the sinless, virgin, New Adam, Jesus was created. This new beginning echoes the original beginning in reverse: rather than Eve being formed from Adam, the New Adam is formed from the sinless New Eve.

Notice that these divine actions occur after Mary is betrothed to Joseph. Only *after* Mary and Joseph entered into a covenant with God and with one another by means of the first stage of Jewish marriage, the betrothal, does God grant the conception of the Word made flesh within the Virgin's sacred womb.[17] The significance of this truth cannot be overstated. Hence, St. Matthew records the angel's words to Joseph during the dream of his own annunciation,

---

17 St. Augustine said, "Here is another of [the heretic's] calumnies, 'Through Joseph,' they say, 'the generations of Christ are counted, and not through Mary.' 'This should not have through Joseph,' they say. Why not through Joseph? Was not Joseph Mary's husband? 'No, they say.' Who says so? For Scripture says on the authority of an angel that he was her husband." *Joseph and Jesus: A Theological Study of Their Relationship, p 38.*

"Do not fear to take Mary *thy wife*" (Mt 1:20 emphasis added).

The impact and effect of this truth has been eclipsed and restricted by an erroneous translation of Mary's response to the angel: "How can this be, since I have no husband."[18] Mary's response to the angel is literally "How shall this happen, since I do not know man." Her words indicate that she did not have sexual intercourse with Joseph, or any man for that matter. Her response can also imply that the she is "*full of grace*," that is, set apart from fallen humanity. The biblical meaning of the word *know* indicates the idea of intimacy. Mary not *knowing* man indicates that she is unlike mankind because she has no intimate subjective experience of the effects of sin.

The translation, "How can this be, since I have no husband," is a misinterpretation at best, or a perversion at worst, that deprives St. Joseph of his vocational mission and unique role in the plan of salvation. St. Joseph was her husband at the moment of the conception of Jesus, and therefore he is the father of Jesus juridically and virginally.[19] Moreover, by excluding St. Joseph

---

18 This error is contained in many translations including *Young's Literal Translation*, Wymouth New Testament, and the *Revised Standard Version*.

19 St. Augustine, defending St. Joseph's fatherhood said, "Just as this was a marriage without deordination, should not the husband have accepted virginally what the wife virginally brought forth? For just as she was virginally the wife, so was he virginally the husband; and just as she was virginally the mother, so was he virginally the father." And again, "Let his greater purity confirm his fatherhood. . . . We should count through Joseph, because as he was virginally the husband, so was he virginally the father." *Joseph and Jesus: A Theological Study of Their*

from his proper role as the icon of God the Father, a subliminal message is communicated, namely that the human father's participation in the family, as symbolized and embodied by St. Joseph, is viewed as ancillary, or worse as unneeded.

Nevertheless, the fact that the conception of the Word made flesh occurred after Mary and Joseph's betrothal testifies and proclaims that God intentionally desired that His Son be conceived and born within the context of a virginal marriage.[20]

Why are these reflections on the *New Genesis* so important to the individual modern man? God willed that the Son of God would be conceived *within* the marriage of Mary and Joseph, making Jesus the spiritual Son of Joseph, and Joseph an icon of God the Father to Jesus. By doing this, God is stating his will and intention: just as St. Joseph is an icon of God the Father to Jesus, so also we fathers are called to be icons of God the Father to our children. You, my brother, are summoned by God to

---

Relationship, p 40.

20 Analyzing the nature of marriage, both St. Augustine and St. Thomas always identify it with an "indivisible union of souls," a "union of hearts" with "consent." These elements are found in an exemplary manner in the marriage of Mary and Joseph. At the culmination of the history of salvation, when God reveals his love for humanity through the gift of the Word, it is precisely the marriage of Mary and Joseph that brings to realization in full "freedom" the "spousal gift of self" in receiving and expressing such a love. "In this great undertaking, which is the renewal of all things in Christ, marriage—it too purified and renewed—becomes a new reality, a sacrament of the New Covenant" (RC, 7).

be a living symbol of his fatherhood, to be a father who exercises and exemplifies the paternal authority of God the Father.

Marriage and the family are not only the foundations of society, but they are the very context in which you, as a man, will learn to love authentically. By responding to the responsibility to be the father and husband within your family, you will ascend from the beasts of the sixth day to the realm of divine sonship of the seventh day, which is marked by communion and intimacy with God.

Your fatherhood, and the way you understand it, embrace it, and live it, is divinely designed to reflect the presence of God the Father's loving authority to your family and the world. This noble responsibility is of the greatest importance and will afford you the true significance for which every man longs.

The Trinity in Humanity

Why did God intentionally wait until after Mary and Joseph had entered the first stage of marriage to proceed with the conception of the Word made flesh?

Some have said that God's intention for the conception of Jesus within the context of marriage was to ensure that Mary would avoid the scandal of being a single mother by having St. Joseph occupy the position and role of being her husband.

THE MEANING AND MYSTERY OF MAN

Or, that St. Joseph's role as husband of Mary granted him the noble responsibly of serving the Virgin Mother and the Son of God, without which they would have certainly struggled to survive. Others propose that by being Mary's husband before the conception of Jesus, St. Joseph was given the legal right to confer the Davidic kingship to Jesus.

Though these reasons are true and valid, they are deductions based on motives whose character is more practical than theological. These reasons are certainly in keeping with human practices and are, humanly speaking, necessary. But perhaps there is a more fundamental, theological reason for Jesus' conception within the context of the holy virgin couple's marriage.

That which is theological is expressed in the practical, and that which is practical should find its fulfillment in that which is theological. God's intentions cannot be reduced to providing practical solutions to man's quandaries, although, by His tender mercy, they often do accomplish such intentions. God ultimately desires that all men experience and share His glory. This truth is the theological underpinning for our Lord's conception within Mary and Joseph's marriage: God desires to share his glory with man, even now on earth.

What then is God's glory? God's glory is His power. His

power is His eternal capacity to love. His love is an eternal exchange of Persons who are a perfect unity of self-giving—a perfect exchange of divine Persons.

God's essence and His glory is unfettered, perfectly disinterested, and infinite self-giving love. "God himself is an eternal exchange of love, Father, Son and Holy Spirit, and he has destined us to share in this exchange" (*CCC*, 221). This eternal unity of love is the fountain from which creation flows, and by which His glory, power, and love are expressed.

Though it be impossible for fallen man to fully comprehend that the eternal exchange of divine Persons is God's glory, it is perhaps possible for man to deduce a sliver of this reality *via negativa*. Consider that the greatest challenge for any man is to overcome selfishness, love disinterestedly, and produce an ongoing perfect union with another human being. Indeed, without God, it is impossible for man to love like God.

What God is in eternity, He desires to reflect in humanity. The God Who is an eternal exchange of Persons created man and woman, marriage and the family, to be the very context in which His eternal exchange of love could be reflected, relived, and revealed.[21]

---

21 "God became a man and a member of a specific family so that all men and women might be able to become members of the supernaturally-constituted

God willed that the Word became flesh within the marriage of Mary and Joseph for the purpose of creating a human reflection of the Trinity.[22] Without St. Joseph being the husband of Mary at the moment of conception, the Holy Family would not have become a living image of the Trinity, for just as the Trinity has a Father, so also the family has a father in His image.[23]

We see in St. Joseph the importance and vital nature of our own fatherhood: you are a father who is to guard the mystery of the Trinity in your family, and your noble task is to protect and cultivate this divine love to ensure that it takes root and

---

family of God, the Church. This means that each Christian family is a reflection of an eternal mystery, for it is "a communion of persons, a sign and image of the communion of the Father and the Son in the Holy Spirit" (*CCC*, 2205).

22 "The first witnesses of Christ's birth, the shepherds, found themselves not only before the Infant Jesus but also a small family: mother, father and newborn son. God had chosen to reveal himself by being born into a human family and the human family thus became an icon of God! God is the Trinity, he is a communion of love; so is the family despite all the differences that exist between the Mystery of God and his human creature, an expression that reflects the unfathomable Mystery of God as Love. In marriage the man and the woman, created in God's image, become 'one flesh' (Gen 2: 24), that is a communion of love that generates new life. The human family, in a certain sense, is an icon of the Trinity because of its interpersonal love and the fruitfulness of this love." Benedict XVI, Angelus, Feast of the Holy Family (December 27, 2009).

23 "If fatherhood in the natural sense of the word supposes a bond both physical and spiritual, it is possible nonetheless to conceive, in the absence of the physical tie of generation, a spiritual bond which is linked not to an action of nature, but to a direct intervention of God—a bond so perfect as to be the basis for a true fatherhood." *Joseph and Jesus: A Theological Study of Their Relationship, p 133.*

flourishes unto the redemption of souls. This is the foundational cause expressed by our Lord to the Pharisees.

The Disorder of the Ultimate Order

The divinely ordained co-mission given to our first parents, Adam and Eve, was the glorious honor of becoming a created version of the uncreated Trinity. God's intention, from the beginning, was that man and woman—by giving themselves to one another in marriage—would reflect and reveal the uncreated order of God in the created order of man.[24]

Indeed, theirs was a vocation to become a created version of the uncreated God for the purpose that their descendants would experience the fullness of God's glory. Adam and Eve's responsibility was to transmit the image of God to the yet unborn human family. It is highly plausible that if they had assumed this responsibility, by means of their virginal, chaste, selfless union, they would have conceived a third in the original sinless state and, consequently, would have become the first human icon of the Trinity.

---

24 "God created man in His own image and likeness (cf. Gn 1:26–27): calling him to existence through love, He called him at the same time for love. God is love (1 Jn 4:8) and in Himself He lives a mystery of personal loving communion. Creating the human race in His own image and continually keeping it in being, God inscribed in the humanity of man and woman the vocation, and thus the capacity and responsibility, of love and communion (cf. GS, 12). Love is therefore the fundamental and innate vocation of every human being." FC, 11.

This divine plan was interrupted and fractured before the actual conception of the third human person occurred. Indeed, the authentic, self-giving union of the first couple was stopped short before achieving the mirror-like reflection of the uncreated Trinitarian order.

It was here, at this pivotal moment in the drama of the human story, after the two had committed themselves to one another, yet before they achieved a union that conceived human life, that the evil one—with the most cunning, malicious intent—entered the garden and beguiled the woman, who in turn tempted and deceived her husband. It was in this moment that the evil one penetrated their virginal union, divided the couple, and threw them headlong into delusion, impeding them from procreating the untarnished image and likeness of the uncreated God within their human created order.

Rather than the original couple becoming a sign of God's glory, they became a first witness to the shame of sin. Rather than becoming an expression of God's power, they were reduced to slavery to their passions. Instead of exchanging love that bore life, they produced the black fruit of death.

Almost immediately after this fall from grace, the history of mankind witnessed the tragic fruits of death in the couple's first offspring, Cain and Abel.[25] The survivor of this first marriage is Cain, who is notoriously remembered for murdering his brother and becoming the first witness of and accomplice to death. Cain's crime sadly confirms that the family who was once ordained to be a sign and symbol of the Trinity has now become an anti-sign of divine self-giving love.

St. Joseph: A New Adam

In the "fullness of time," at the culmination of the heritage of unfaithful men, God called a man from among men to be singled out as the forerunner of fidelity to the vocation of husbands and fathers as the guardian and keeper—not only of the Virgin Mary and the Son of God—but also of the very imprint of the Trinity upon the human family.[26]

Though, like Adam, St. Joseph was tempted to separate himself from his vocational path,[27] he heroically retraced his steps and

---

25 See Gn 4.

26 "There is, then, no doubt that St. Joseph was endowed with all the graces and all the gifts that were required for the care which the Eternal Father willed to give him of the temporal and domestic economy of our Lord, and of the guidance of His family. This was composed of only three persons, who represent to us the mystery of the most holy and most adorable Trinity; not that there is any comparison except with regard to our Lord, who is one of the Persons of the most Holy Trinity, for the others are creatures. But yet we may say that it is a Trinity on earth, which in a manner represents to us the most Holy Trinity: Mary, Jesus and Joseph; Joseph, Jesus and Mary; a Trinity marvelously estimable and worthy of being honored." Conferences of St. Francis de Sales, Conference 19.

27 See Mt 1:21.

assumed his theological position as *custos*, the guardian and protector of the great mystery of the Trinity in his family.

St. Joseph became what Adam did not: a man who sacrificed himself for—without knowing it—the mystery of the Trinity. Indeed, by virtue of St. Joseph's fidelity to his vocational post, and through his remaining united in fidelity to Mary, he afforded the world the first human archetype and model of the Blessed Trinity, whose fruit was Jesus Christ.

Pope St. John Paul II testifies to the fact that this holy couple's *perfect communion of persons* became a living reflection and real sharing in the Trinity's love for mankind:

> The marriage of Mary and Joseph conceals within itself, at the same time, the mystery of the *perfect communion of persons*, of the man and woman in the conjugal pact, and also the mystery of that singular continence for the kingdom.[28]
>
> The essence and role of the family are in the final analysis specified by love. Hence the family has the mission to guard, reveal and communicate love, and this is a living reflection of and a real sharing in God's love for humanity and the love of Christ the Lord for

---

28   John Paul II, *Theology of the Body*, 268. Hereafter *Theology of the Body*.

the Church his bride."[29] This being the case, it is in the Holy Family, the original: "Church in miniature (*Ecclesia domestica*),"[30] that every Christian family must be reflected. . . . It is therefore the prototype and example for all Christian families.[31] *(Redemptoris Custos, 7)*

By virtue of the Holy Family being the first human reflection of the Trinity, a living reflection and real sharing of God's Trinitarian love, a *New Genesis* has begun in which the uncreated order of love of the Trinity is now expressed concretely within the created order of the human family.

The point is this: the virginal couple, Mary and Joseph, reversed the sin of Adam and Eve. Whereas death came into the world through the first couple, life and redemption came into the world through Mary and Joseph.[32] Jesus, who is grace and truth,[33]

29 *FC*, 100.

30 *Ibid.*, 140; Cf. Second Vatican Council, Dogmatic Constitution on the Church, Lumen Gentium, 11; Decree on the Apostolate of the Laity, *Apostolicam Actuositatem*, 11.

31 *FC*, 189.

32 Regarding the idea of virginal fruitfulness St. Ephrem applied the analogy of the palm tree to symbolize St. Joseph's role in the Incarnation of the Word. "St. Ephrem's idea is based on the legend that male palms are said to make female palm trees fruitful not by contact or by sharing of their substance, but by their mere shadow." *Joseph and Jesus: A Theological Study of Their Relationship*, p 28; See also, St. Ephrem, *Joseph and Jesus: A Theological Study of Their Relationship*, p 28,

33 See Jn 1:14.

is the fruit of their union. Christ's presence flows to the world through the portal of this holy, virginal marriage of Mary and Joseph. Considering this, we can conclude that all grace flows in an ongoing manner to humanity through this perfect union of Mary and Joseph in the Person of Jesus Christ by the Holy Spirit "for the gifts and the call of God are irrevocable"[34] and "what God has brought together, let no man divide" (Mk 10:9).

By virtue of the Holy Family, baptized members who constitute a family now have the power and potential to be a perpetual sign that awakens mankind to the Trinity's eternal self-giving love.

The New Genesis

Without considering the content and context of the fall of Adam or the reason for the magnitude of the consequential damage it has caused the human race, it will be of great benefit for us to return to Genesis. By revisiting the disobedience of Adam and Eve, we discover in the couple a typological precursor of the *New Genesis* of faith found in Mary and Joseph. By studying this new beginning in St. Joseph, we will derive great insight, guidance, and a renewed hope in our pursuit of penetrating the

---

34 Cf. Gn 3:1–11; Rom 5:19.

mystery of man, and the mystery of ourselves as men.

Recall that it was Adam and Eve, the first parents of our race, who, by their mutual disobedience to God the Father, submitted to the serpent's temptation and thereby gave birth to death.

> Man, tempted by the devil, let his trust in his Creator die in his heart and, abusing his freedom, disobeyed God's command. This is what man's first sin consisted of. All subsequent sin would be disobedience toward God and lack of trust in his goodness. (*CCC*, 397)

The first virgin, sinless couple's parentage transmitted the curse of disintegration between man and woman, between the body and the soul, between mankind and God.[35]

---

35 "The account of the fall in *Genesis 3* uses figurative language, but affirms a primeval event, a deed that took place *at the beginning of the history of man* (cf. GS, 13 §1). Revelation gives us the certainty of faith that the whole of human history is marked by the original fault freely committed by our first parents" (cf. Council of Trent: DS 1513; Pius XII: DS 3897; Paul VI: AAS 58 (1966), 654). CCC, 390; "The harmony in which they had found themselves, thanks to original justice, is now destroyed: the control of the soul's spiritual faculties over the body is shattered; the union of man and woman becomes subject to tensions, their relations henceforth marked by lust and domination (cf. Gn 3:7–16). Harmony with creation is broken: visible creation has become alien and hostile to man (cf. Gn 3:17,19). Because of man, creation is now subject 'to its bondage to decay' (Rom 8:21). Finally, the consequence explicitly foretold for this disobedience will come true: man will 'return to the ground,' (Gn 3:19; cf. 2:17) for out of it he was taken. *Death makes its entrance into human history*" (cf. Rom 5:12). *CCC*, 400.

The word *origin*, used in Matthew's genealogy of Jesus "can be translated even more specifically as the parentage of Jesus Christ."[36] Whereas Adam and Eve's parentage was one of death, the content of Joseph and Mary's virginal parentage was Jesus Christ—the author of life.

In the fullness of time, this virginal couple, through mutual obedience to and trust in God, and a profound union of wills,[37] brought forth divine life and redemption to a world bound by the consequences of sin.[38] This virginal couple's submission to one another and to God constitutes a new beginning, a new economy of grace, which reversed the end (death and damnation) of the original beginning into a new beginning that leads and directs humanity to the ultimate end.

We see that at the beginning of the New Testament, as at the beginning of the Old, there is a married couple. But whereas Adam and Eve were the source of evil that was unleashed on the world,

---

36 L. Cantwell Cardiff, "The Parentage of Jesus, MT 1:18–21," *Novum Testamentum* XXIV (1982), 304–305.

37 See *RC*, 7: Indivisible union of wills, union of souls found in an exemplary way in the marriage of Joseph and Mary.

38 "The marriage of Mary and Joseph conceals within itself, at the same time, the mystery of the perfect communion of the persons, of the man and woman in the conjugal pact, and also the mystery of that singular continence for the kingdom of heaven: a continence that served, in the history of salvation, the most perfect 'fruitfulness of the holy Spirit.' Indeed, it was in a certain sense the absolute fullness of that spiritual fruitfulness since precisely in marriage . . . there was realize the gift of the incarnation." *Theology of the Body*, 268.

Joseph and Mary are the summit from which holiness spreads over all the earth. The Savior began the work of salvation by this virginal holy union, wherein is manifested his all-powerful will to purify and sanctify the family—that sanctuary and cradle of life.[39]

The Purpose of This Work

My brother, not only will our reflections on the role of the original man enable us to consider in depth God's original plan for marriage and family, but these reflections will enable us to mine the profound riches of each man's vocation, which culminates in spiritual fatherhood.

As mentioned previously, the task of this body of work is to compare Adam and St. Joseph, and by linking St. Joseph to Jesus—the eternal fulfillment of Adam—we will discover the glory and meaning of man in clearer light.

Indeed, St. Joseph is a hinge, a bridge, which connects the original Adam with the New Adam, Jesus Christ. To understand and comprehend Christ, our original dignity as men, and our noble calling as fathers in Christ, we will meditate upon this comparison at length. By means of these reflections we will not only uncover more of the mystery and meaning of the universal

---

39   Paul VI, Discourse (May 4, 1970).

man, but also our personal mystery, identity, and destiny: to be like St. Joseph and his Son—fathers in the image of God the Father and sons in the image of the eternally divine Son. Let us, my brother, "Go to Joseph, and what he says, you do" (Gn 41:55).

CHAPTER 2

The Guardian of the Garden

DEFINING MAN'S POSITION IN GOD'S PLAN

Then Jesus was led by the spirit into the desert, to be
tempted by the devil.

—Matthew 4:1

Temptation: A Means to Salvation

Temptation will either crush you or help to sanctify you.
You, my brother, will be led into various temptations but
let not temptation lead you.

The One who taught His disciples to pray "[Father] lead us
not into temptation" (Mt 6:13) was led by the Holy Spirit into
temptation.[40]

---

40 See Mt 4:1.

God tempts no one,[41] but rather allows us to be led into temptation, that is, the spiritual battle because man must prove that he loves the God who has proven His love for man. The Holy Spirit leads man into combat with the devil, who can only be conquered by love. Overcoming temptation is a proof of love for only love animated by faith can overcome temptation truly.[42] "The greatest of all evils is not to be tempted, because there are then grounds for believing that the devil looks upon us as his property."[43]

Temptations can be likened to the ocean tide, which is relentless, pounding, and never-ending. The ocean's waves will never cease crashing upon earth's shoreline, nor will temptations cease crashing upon the shores of man's soul. The choice is yours, my brother, whether you will be sand, saturated by and washed into the tide of temptation, or rock that repels the waters of temptation, while allowing its character to be shaped by them. "Truly I tell you that no one should consider himself a perfect friend of God until he has passed through many temptations and tribulations"[44]

---

41 See Jas 1:13–15.

42 "For love of God is this, that we keep his commandments." 1 Jn 5:3.

43 St. John Vianney, *Wisdom of the Saints* (New York, New York: Barnes and Noble, 2004).

44 St. Francis de Sales, *Wisdom of the Saints* (New York, New York: Barnes and Noble, 2004).

Temptation can lead to salvation,[45] for if a man encounters temptation and rises above it, he has increased his capacity to love for he learns to have compassion on those who are being tempted in the very ways that he has experienced temptation.[46]

Even if a man succumbs to temptation and repents of his sin, he can benefit from his repentance by growing in humility and receiving the Lord's mercy.[47] Because of the mercy he has received, he will be more capable to give mercy to those in need. Therefore, "count it all joy, when you fall into divers temptations: Knowing that the trying of your faith worketh patience. And patience hath a perfect work: that you may be perfect and entire, failing in nothing" (Jas 1:2–3).

If a soldier does not set out for battle, the battle will come to him. To be led out onto the horizon of battle is to keep the battle and the enemy at bay, away from one's domain. If temptation is allowed to enter your soul—to the point of being considered—

---

45 "Our pilgrimage on earth cannot be exempt from trial. We progress by means of trial. No one knows himself except through trial, or receives a crown except after victory, or strives except against an enemy or temptations." St. Augustine.
46 See 2 Cor 1:4.
47 "Sin is shameful only when we commit it; but, being converted into confession and penance, it becomes honorable and wholesome—contrition and confession being so beautiful and odoriferous as to efface its deformity and purify its stench." St. Francis de Sales, *Introduction to the Devout Life* (New York: Frederick Pustet & Co).

the battle has entered your domain, and, in fact, you have all but surrendered yourself and your domain.

In the beginning, the sacred writer of the creation account tells us:

> The Lord God formed man of the slime of the earth; and breathed unto his face the breath of life, and man became a living soul. And the Lord God had planted a paradise of pleasure from the beginning: wherein he placed man whom he had formed. (Genesis 2:7–8)

And again:

> And the Lord God took man, and put him into the paradise of pleasure, to dress it, and keep it. (Genesis 2:15)

A common misconception of the creation of man is that God formed him in the garden of paradise. God created man outside of the garden, not in it.[48] It seems that the Holy Spirit divinely inspired the sacred writer to highlight the fact—not once, but

---

48 See Gn 2:7, 15.

twice for the purpose of reinforcing the importance of this truth—that the first man was created outside of the garden.

This double emphasis can be likened to our Lord's double Amen: "Amen, amen, I say to you,"[49] meaning listen, for what will be said is of tremendous importance. Indeed, my brother, by examining the idea that God formed the man outside of the garden, we will be enlightened regarding the mystery and meaning of man.

God created Adam from the "slime of the earth (adamah)" (Gn 2:7). Adam's origin begins in the uncharted, undiscovered, undomesticated wilderness, outside of the garden of paradise. Adam is forever connected to his roots—the adamah.

From these insights, we glean the idea that within the soul of Adam and the souls of the sons of Adam is an innate instinct to navigate, discover, and exercise dominion over the unknown, undiscovered world. Man's instinct is to till and use the earth for the purpose of discovering himself, his origins, and the reason for his existence. By digging into the earth, man, metaphorically, is digging into himself.[50]

---

49   E.g., Jn 10:1.

50   Leon Kass, "Man and Woman: An Old Story," *First Things* (November 1991), 17 is constituted by two principles, one low ("dust of the earth") and one high ("breath of life"). The human being first comes to sight as a formed and animated (or breathing) dust of the ground. Higher than the earth, yet still bound to it, the human being has a name, Adam (from *adamah*, meaning "earth" or "ground"), which reminds him of his lowly terrestrial origins. Man is, from the start, up from below and in between.

THE MEANING AND MYSTERY OF MAN

Subconsciously, man continually returns to the *adamah*, not only to discover himself, but also to discover and encounter the God who formed him from the earth. Man tills the earth, subdues it, and brings forth its fruit, which is a symbol of life, in imitation of the God who raised him to life from the earth.

At this point, man is *outside* the garden, which will eventually become the stage and context for his God-given mission and personal battle. Only after breathing the breath of life into Adam's nostrils, and only after giving him a soul, does God take this outsider and place him inside the garden, commanding him to dress and protect it. By receiving these commands to dress and protect the garden, the man intuited that an enemy exists from whom he must protect himself and his domain.[51]

Eden, the English rendition of the Hebrew word (the name of the Garden) can be interpreted as delight or luxury. The garden is a symbol of the context where man will experience joy and delight. Yet, the garden is also the place where grave temptation will occur.

---

51 By God giving Adam the commands to protect and cherish the garden, while also indicating that the consequence of eating the forbidden fruit will incur death, Adam became aware that 1) an enemy exists from whom the garden must be protected and 2) death is a reality. Lucifer's fall from Heaven was prior to the creation account, and therefore the existence of sin was also prior to the creation of Adam. Sin and death go hand-in-hand. Lucifer, the devil, sins and thereby death becomes a real factor. Lucifer's sin does not constitute the Original Sin of man but was an influential factor contributing to it.

God intentionally sets Adam in the context of trial, the setting wherein temptation will occur—not to tempt or seduce him—but not without warning. Though the garden is a paradise, it is also the perennial setting for battle, precisely because it is a paradise, a symbol of Heaven, and for this reason the devil is determined to destroy it. "By the envy of the devil, death came to the world" (Wis 2:24).

The Garden: Place of Paradise and Battle

Occasionally, the word garden in the Old Testament is used to symbolize woman, her fruitfulness, and her interior mystery as in the Songs of Songs: "You are a garden enclosed a fountain sealed, my sister, my bride" (Sg 4:12).

The garden is a rich symbol of woman, the children she bears, her mystery, and the domestic domain. Woman is a "garden enclosed" in that her virginity and her fruitfulness is her own, and it is not to be plundered by the lusts of men. She is a "fountain sealed" because her fruitfulness, the fountain of life, is "sealed up," contained within her, until she decides to open herself to the husband who can make her fruitful.[52]

---

52 "The 'sister bride' is for the man the master of her own mystery as a 'garden enclosed' and a 'fountain sealed.' The language of the body reread in truth keeps pace with the discovery of the interior inviolability of the person." *Theology of the Body*, 110.

With this in mind, the words *dress* and *keep* have profound significance. The Hebrew word for dress, *abad,* means to cherish. Adam is to hold dear and to cultivate with care and affection the garden that has been entrusted to him. Far from simply accepting the garden, he is to uphold its dignity and intrinsic value. Man must move from mere receptive acceptance of the gift to choosing the gift as his cherished own.

Being that there is a symbolic connection between the garden and the woman, this command evokes a profound connection between it and the universal need for wives to be cherished by their husbands as St. Paul expresses in his Letter to the Ephesians.[53] It is necessary that God commands the man to cherish the garden because man takes for granted, not only the goodness of the created world, but also the goodness of woman and woman's Creator.

Certainly, it is a great challenge for a husband to express profound, ongoing gratitude for his wife by caring for her with deep affection. In addition to this, the Hebrew word for keep, *shamar,* means to protect. Adam is given the mission to protect the garden that he cherishes, which is not only a place but also a figure of the woman.

---

53 See Eph 5.

Considering these insights, we begin to penetrate the mystery of why man is never completely at home in the garden. His soul is not completely settled while living in the domestic setting. Man, symbolized by Adam, has one foot in the external, uncharted, and perhaps hostile world, while the other foot is planted in the mystery, richness, and fruitfulness of domestic love. Only by connecting the mystery of the outside world with the mystery of the interior, domestic world will man discover the external, eternal God within his internal, mortal being.

While enduring his earthly existence, man's soul is pulled between the tensions of the external world and the interior garden. Therefore, while being outside of the garden, he longs for the warmth and comfort of marital, familial love, safety, sustenance, and rest. Yet, while participating in domestic life, he grows restless, desiring the next challenge, conquest, and adventure.

This tension is willed by God. Adam and all men have the task to stand on the horizon between the outside world and the realm of domestic life. The sacred summons of every man is to integrate both of these worlds, while always ensuring that evil not be permitted to enter the garden.

Too often, especially while living in a culture of toleration and inclusion, we are conditioned to believe that integration of the secular and sacred, the external and internal, entails an engulfing of the sacred by the secular; the garden being overrun by the wild.

The man's noble duty is to hunt, develop, and gather the fruits from the outside world and bring them to his family without allowing the weeds of evil to re-seed themselves in his interior garden. Man must remember that he is continually at war and that his enemy is bent on plundering his house. Animated by God, man is to sanctify the secular, rather than secularizing the sacred. It is crucial that man assume his post as guardian of the garden, cherishing it and protecting it, lest it be invaded, overrun, and destroyed.

Faulting at His Post

Man is forever outside the mystery of the garden, while simultaneously being divinely summoned to actively participate within it. In sexual relations, man enters the woman's "garden" and plants his seed. From that point onward, he remains outside of the mystery of the child forming within its mother, yet he is continually summoned to participate in this mystery.[54]

The husband is "other," outside of the mystery of motherhood; yet, he is responsible for cherishing and defending this

---

54 "The man—even with all his sharing in parenthood—always remains 'outside' the process of pregnancy and the baby's birth; in many ways he has to learn his own 'fatherhood' from the mother. . . . The mother's contribution is decisive in laying the foundation for a new human personality." *MD*, 18.

mystery at all cost. Being stationed outside of the mystery of the garden gives the man a certain edge. He is capable of thinking prudentially in moments of danger or in decisions that demand protection at the cost of worldly relationships. Indeed, protection of the sacred interior garden is primary over the task of engaging the outside world peaceably.

There is a tendency for sons of Adam who feel disconnected from the mystery of the domestic life to return to the outside world and remain there. His hobbies, adventures, initiatives, and labors—though at the onset appear to be at the service of the mystery of the garden—can easily dominate his attention and lure him from his post as leader, defender, and lover of his family.

If man's primary attention is given to the exterior world, he will forever distance himself from his God-given subjects, while also distancing his subjects, and himself, from God.

The restless son of Adam finds solace in the labors of his hands—and rightfully so—for they are a symbol of the mystery of the unfolding of God's creation. Indeed, man's creativity helps to link the creature to the mystery of the Creator and His creativity. Yet, man's creativity can become a distraction, an idol that lures him from his true vocation of tilling and keeping the garden of his family.

On the other hand, a son of Adam can become too settled in the garden, too comfortable with the domestic life, and henceforth neglect to venture into the challenging, competitive, uncharted world with the purpose of mining its resources for the sake of his family and claiming proper dominion over creation. He fears combat with the enemy more than the risk of failing his family and, therefore, risks becoming domesticated, effeminate, and lacking virtue and perseverance. He consistently avoids the rigorous and arduous work demanded of him to bring order to a disordered world, to enhance the sacred by the use of the secular, while injecting the secular with the sacred.

Considering this, the man who primarily dwells in the garden, while *consistently avoiding the challenge to enter the exterior competitive world*, will cling to woman,[55] become overly submissive to her, and depend on her for his identity. By looking to woman for his identity, he will burden her, and being burdened she will become his burden.

If the man continually looks "inside" to his wife for a disordered type of validation, she will eventually peer beyond his effeminacy to the "outside" for affirmation. The seed of this dynamic is hinted

---

55   Here, we are not speaking of the man, who by prudential decision has decided to remain at home while his wife, because of her gifts, talents and capabilities enables her to obtain income for the family, but the man who avoids and neglects work in a spirit of sloth and pusillanimity.

at in the Fall of Eve. When the secular invades the sacred, the man's unwillingness to defend his wife will inadvertently drive her to desire a man of the wild, who appears to be a protector.

St. Joseph: Guardian of the Garden of Mary

In the Gospel of St. Matthew, we first encounter St. Joseph in solitude and perplexity after discovering that his betrothed, Mary, is pregnant without his cooperation. It is within Mary, the celestial garden,[56] that the seed of the Incarnate Word of God was divinely planted, while St. Joseph himself remained outside of this august mystery.

Indeed, after being confronted with the virgin's pregnancy, St. Joseph separated himself from this confounding situation, dwelling in a personal, wilderness of solitude. Yet, God commanded St. Joseph, through an angelic intermediary, to "fear not to take unto thee Mary thy wife" (Mt 1:20). Here, we discover a valuable insight. It was God who placed the original Adam in the garden, and it was God who commanded St. Joseph to protect the garden of Mary.

These events support the idea that woman is not an object or a prize that man apprehends by his initiative. Man must

---

56 St. Louis de Montfort, *True Devotion to Mary* (Rockford, Il, TAN Books and Publishers, Inc., 1985).

wait upon God to grant him permission to enter her garden; hence the meaning of a "garden enclosed and fountain sealed." Far more than a biological, instinctual, automated response to woman's beauty, the summons to enter the garden of woman is a divine calling and must be respected as such. The man demonstrates to God that he respects this divine call by respecting the woman and awaiting her consent. This waiting is at the service of purifying the man of his lustful or inordinate desires.

> Man must learn "to be the true master of his own deep impulses, like a guardian who watches over a hidden spring; and finally, to draw from those impulses what is fitting for 'purity of heart.'"[57]

St. Joseph feared the idea of "taking" Mary as his wife. Indeed, he refused to *take* her. St. Joseph, rather than taking the woman, waited with humble receptivity before God. Considering this, we can deduce that a woman is not to be mastered by a man's desire. Rather a man must master his desire for the woman. He is to strive to overcome lust, rather than allow lust to overtake him.[58]

---

57 *Theology of the Body*, 172.
58 "The 'language of the body' reread in truth keeps pace with the discovery of the interior inviolability of the person." *Theology of the Body*, 372, 373.

Seeking the permission of God, and permission from the woman, heightens the man's respect for the woman, the "garden enclosed," thus inspiring him to cherish her with affection and care. A man protects that which he cherishes. St. Joseph refused to expose Mary to shame [59] because he cherished her, even above himself and his desire for a wife. In other words, St. Joseph protected Mary—even from himself. Indeed, the scripture, "He that has confidence in his own heart is a fool; but he who walks wisely, he shall be delivered" (Prv 28:26), can be applied appropriately to St. Joseph.

As the Lord God placed Adam in the garden, in a similar way, God commanded St. Joseph to stand on the horizon between the external world and the mystery of Mary, "*the* garden enclosed and *the* fountain sealed."

Artistic renderings often depict St. Joseph as sleeping when the angel commanded him to take unto himself Mary his wife. Though the perplexed St. Joseph's sleep can be easily misinterpreted as "sleeping on the job," nevertheless, the portrayal is beneficial for men in that St. Joseph can represent the man who has fallen asleep regarding his true mission as guardian of the garden. We must be clear: St. Joseph did not neglect his vocation. Indeed, such a man must awaken to his true and noble calling by re-engaging

---

59   See Mt 1:19.

himself continually. The heroic husband, symbolized by St. Joseph, is called by God to re-engage himself and re-enter the garden.

One can safely say that the devil assailed St. Joseph with the temptation to remain on the "outside" of the mystery unfolding in Mary, which is his methodology with most, if not all, men.[60] Yet, St. Joseph, aided by the grace of God, resisted the temptation to withdraw from the Holy Virgin and heroically retraced his steps, returning to his post as guardian of *the* garden enclosed.

In a similar way, the devil is bent on driving you from your vocational post as guardian of your garden that he may have his way with your wife and children. Indeed, his intent is to bind you, the strong man of your house, to plunder your family.[61] The evil one's intention is the destruction of the Christian family, the domestic church, for it is there that Christ is conceived spiritually

---

60 Temptation is not to be confused with sin or the participation in the act of sin. Being tempted does not nullify the righteous character of the man, in this case St. Joseph, but rather, by his overcoming the temptation, his just character is elevated and highlighted more prominently.

61 "No man can enter into the house of a strong man and rob him of his goods, unless he first bind the strong man, and then shall he plunder his house." Mk 3:27; The strong man Christ was referring to was the devil, who due to the infidelity of the Jewish priests and elders, possessed the Temple. The strong man is the devil to whom Christ will bind and then plunder the Temple claiming it as his Father's house. We see this physically demonstrated in the act of His cleansing of the Temple. Though this is the literal interpretation we can also apply the metaphor to the human father who can be the strong man that the devil is intent on binding for the purpose of dividing the family, overthrowing the mother, and devouring the child.

ever anew. "The devil is prowling around like a lion, looking for someone to devour. Resist him. Steadfast in your faith" (1 Pt 5:8). You, my brother, are to continually re-engage yourself in the battle to overcome the temptation to flee from your post. This demands faith, a supernatural trust in God that He will supply you with the will and desire to protect your family at all cost. If your wife and children are to be preserved from evil and remain secure in their journey toward Heaven, it is imperative that you, as the strong man of your house, stand your ground and resist the devil.

Jesus Christ: The Guardian of the Garden

Promptly after His baptism in the Jordan River by St. John the Baptist, Jesus, the New Adam, is led by the Holy Spirit into the wilderness to be tempted by the devil for forty days.[62]

Though the wilderness is a physical place it also serves as a symbol of the garden of paradise displaying the full effect of Original Sin. Metaphorically, the garden has become a fruitless wilderness due to mankind's sins. The wilderness represents spiritual dryness and, perhaps at times, a lack of the presence of God.

Our Lord launches out into the wilderness to engage in the spiritual battle to reclaim and redeem that which was stolen by

---

62   See Lk 4:1.

the devil. He brings His divine Presence into the hostile world. Here, in the wild, the Lord Jesus assumes his position as the "outside man," injecting His divine presence into all of creation with the intention of reclaiming it that it may become a fruitful garden.

Later in Jesus' life, on the night of His betrayal, He enters a garden and undergoes a severe, heartrending agony. The Garden of Gethsemane was described by the evangelists as the meeting place for Jesus and His Apostles and served as a refuge of safety and respite for the Master and His disciples.[63] Indeed, the Garden of Gethsemane is a compelling symbol of the fruitful interior life where one encounters the mystery of God in Christ.

In the Garden of Gethsemane, the outside hostile world and the interior life of the garden collided as the cohort, led by the betrayer Judas Iscariot, attempted to invade and trample the garden.[64] Jesus, "knowing all things that should come upon him, *went forth* and said to them: Whom seek ye?" (Jn 18:4, emphasis added).

The Lord Jesus, the defender of His future Church represented by His Apostles—symbolized mystically by the garden—went

---

63 "And Judas also, who betrayed him, knew the place; because Jesus had often resorted thither together with his disciples." Jn 18:2.

64 "Judas therefore having received a band of soldiers and servants from the chief priests and the Pharisees, cometh thither with lanterns and torches and weapons." Jn 18:3.

forth to protect his disciples from being overtaken. "If therefore you seek me, let these go their way" (Jn 18:8).

The Greek root word for agony is *ago*, which means to be led into challenge or competition. The garden becomes the setting for our Lord's great challenge. It is here, within the garden, that Jesus steps forth to keep the devil, embodied by the betrayer and his ilk, at bay, away from his Apostles.

Our Lord, as the definitive fulfillment of Adam,[65] assumed his position as guardian of the garden, standing on the horizon between the outside wilderness and the interior garden, overcoming the temptation to remain silent and withdraw from his sacrifice. The Savior pressed forward unwaveringly, courageously surrendering himself to his enemy for the purpose of saving and defending the Bride, His Church, and his future faithful.

The perfect integration of the outside man and inside man in the Person of Jesus Christ can be expressed most vividly in His incarnation. The eternal Word becoming man encapsulates the reality of the eternal outside Word, whose longing to save and redeem man compels Him to enter inside creation, inside the womb of the Virgin Mother, and permanently become one of humanity's own children, enabling the sons of men to become sons of God.

---

65 See Rom 5:12–18.

From Christ we learn that to move from the outside secular world to the inside garden always demands a radical humility by which we lower ourselves beneath the other for the sake of raising the other to God.

The Sacred Summons

My brother, as with Adam, St. Joseph, and the Lord Jesus, God has created you to stand on the horizon between the hostile world and the interior garden of the domestic life. This is your position in the spiritual combat. Your family—though at times it may be difficult to perceive—is the hope of the future Church and, therefore, the hope of the world. It is your noble task to be the guardian of this garden and to ensure that no evil overrun or overtake it.

The devil stands poised to conquer the woman and devour her child,[66] and you stand in the breech between the woman and her nemesis. Our Lord's words confirm the human father's singular position and role: "No man can enter into the house of a strong man and rob him of his goods, unless he first binds the strong man, and then shall he plunder his house" (Mk 3:27). Though our Lord was referring to the house of the Temple in

---

66 See Rev 12:5.

Jerusalem and the strong man, the devil who possessed it, this passage applies to both the father of lies and the human father.

The evil one is waging war on your family with the evil intent of binding you, the strong man, to ensure that he is able to slither his way into the garden of your domestic life and plunder your wife and children. This is his aim and intention.

The Lord of creation continually places man in the crucible of the garden to forge him into a true man who can glorify God and, in glorifying God, be glorified by God. Indeed, "He hath called you by our gospel, unto the purchasing of the glory of our Lord Jesus Christ" (2 Thes 2:13). God has created you for this mission and battle. The fact that you are from the "outside" gives you a certain ability to go forth as Christ did and combat the devil, the flesh, and the world while also standing your ground, and cherishing and defending the mystery of the Trinity in your family.

This mission demanded Christ's life and, in a similar way, your mission will demand your willingness to sacrifice your life for others that the life of Christ in others may not be sacrificed.

CHAPTER 3

Man's Role and Responsibility

THE HIERARCHY OF SACRIFICIAL RESPONSIBILITY

> No man taketh [my life] away from me: but I lay it down
> of myself, and I have the power to take it up again. This
> commandment have I received of my Father.
>
> —John 10:18

Unique Roles, Equal Dignity

Equality is not sameness. Uniformity is not unity. Uniformity means remaining the same in all cases at all times or unchanging in form or character. Though uniformity may appear to be unified, it rarely inculcates or fosters true unity.

Unity, the state of being joined to form a whole, indicates that a part is not complete until it is joined to its completing part. The reason that uniformity does not foster unity ultimately is because all who are the same in form or character have no need for another for the purpose of completing themselves. More of the same thing does not complete the something or the same thing.

Man and woman are not uniform, yet they are called to unity. Man and woman are not the same but are equal. They have the same dignity and equality without ever being the same. To reduce the roles and responsibilities of man and woman as being the same is an attempt to create uniformity among, rather than unity between, man and woman.

Man and woman's sexual and ontological differences demonstrate that they are not the same; and, if they are not the same, their roles and responsibilities—though they overlap and are similar—should not be regarded as the same. If the man and woman's roles and responsibilities are the same, then they have no real need for the other for they are uniform rather than being unified. Yet, man and woman are not the same, but rather they are equal in dignity. The man and woman's role and responsibilities complement and complete one another to form a whole.[67]

---

[67] "I would define a man as a human being who both gives in a receiving way and receives in a giving way, but is so structured in his being that he is emphatically inclined toward giving in a receiving way. The nature of being a man is an emphasis on giving in a receiving way. A woman is a human being who both gives in a receiving way and receives in a giving way, but is so structured in her being that she is emphatically inclined toward receiving in a giving way. The nature of being a woman is an emphasis on receiving in a giving way. . . . The sexuality of man and woman . . . is orientated in opposite but very complementary

The incessant efforts to make man and woman the same, that is uniform, has clouded the reality of man and woman's relationship and their roles and responsibilities to such a degree that many men no longer know what it means to truly be a man.

By making the woman the same as the man, rather than elevating her, she has been robbed of her unique and unrepeatable genius that is exclusively hers.

Efforts to deny the man of his unique genius has made him more like a woman yet without her motherly creative power.

Not only have the promotion of women's rights frequently led to the diminishment of the rights of the man, but also to a reduction of the woman herself, pressuring her to assume a pseudo-masculine character rather than experiencing the glory and dignity of her feminine genius.[68]

---

ways." Robert E. Joyce, *Human Sexual Ecology: A Philosophy and Ethics of Man and Woman* (Washington: University Press of America, 1980), 70–71.

68 "Therefore the Church can and should help modern society by tirelessly insisting that the work of women in the home be recognized and respected by all in its irreplaceable value. . . . While it must be recognized that women have the same right as men to perform various public functions, society must be structured in such a way that wives and mothers are not in practice compelled to work outside the home, and that their families can live and prosper in a dignified way even when they themselves devote their full time to their own family. Furthermore, the mentality which honors women more for their work outside the home than for their work within the family must be overcome. This requires that men should truly esteem and love women with total respect for their personal dignity, and that society should create and develop conditions favoring work in the home." *FC*, 23.

This dynamic, to a great degree, has feminized a great number of men, convincing them that their masculinity should be masked, and most certainly never imposed upon the world.

In pursuit of equality, the modern culture attempts to elevate the woman by diminishing the man; and, by diminishing the man, he no longer senses a need to protect, cherish, and elevate the woman for she has elevated herself—or has been elevated—at the cost of him.

Rather than raising the sexes to new heights, modern equality reduces the two to the lowest common denominator, which by its very action divides their power rather than multiplies it.

By means of their sexual complementarity, true women assist men in becoming real men, and true men assist women in becoming great women. In other words, a woman is not a man, but a woman can help a man become a true man. A man is not a woman but can help the woman become a true woman. A mother is not a father; nor is a father a mother; yet the woman can help the man become a true father, and the man can help the woman become a true mother. On the other hand, the attempt to interchange the sexes diffuses and reduces the power of true equality in unity.

What then is man's unique role and responsibility? How does it complement and help complete the woman, elevating her to her fullest capacity?

Sacrificial Responsibility

Returning to the ancient creation account, we discover a clue to man's unique and vital role in God's plan of salvation, though this clue is often overlooked and rarely mentioned:

> And the Lord God took man, and put him into the paradise of pleasure, to dress, and to keep it. And He commanded him, saying: Of every tree of paradise you shall eat: But of the tree of knowledge of good and evil, thou shalt not eat. For in what day soever thou shalt eat of it, thou shalt die the death. And the Lord God said: It is not good for man to be alone: let us make him a help like unto himself. (Genesis 2:15–18)

It is common for readers of the two Genesis creation accounts to conclude that God charged both Adam and Eve directly with the command to not eat from the Tree of Knowledge of Good and Evil. However, examining the text more closely, it appears that this may not be the case. According to the second creation account, the woman did not yet exist when God gave the man the commands regarding the garden.

From the outset, God communicated to Adam the responsibility of keeping the divine command; and implicit is the fact that it was Adam's responsibility to not only obey the command but to communicate this command to his future spouse that she may keep it also.[69]

By giving Adam the "definitive commandment" and implicitly giving him the responsibility to communicate this command to Eve, God was establishing a hierarchal order of sacrificial responsibility. Indeed, man is responsible to God for the woman.

"Although the maintenance of the balance of the gift seems to have been entrusted to both [man and woman], a special responsibility rests with the man above all, as if it depended more on him whether this balance is maintained or broken, or even—if already broke—re-established."[70]

How often is this truth contested and rejected by those who interpret the message as being misogynistic, or understood as a diminution of woman or as categorizing her in a lower classification than the man, which is clearly a grave misinterpretation.

This idea of masculine sacrificial responsibility is emphasized by the fact that after Adam and Eve's act of disobeying the command and their consequential fall from grace, God does

---

69   "But of the tree of knowledge of good and evil, thou shalt not eat. For in what day soever thou shalt eat of it, thou shalt die the death." Gn 2:17.

70   *Theology of the Body*, 128–129.

not initially address the one who sinned first (the woman), but rather the one who was first given the command (the man).

Further evidence of man's hierarchal position of sacrificial responsibility is derived from the words addressed to the man by God: "Where are you?"[71] God did not ask Adam, "What have you done?" or, "Who are you?" but rather, "Where are you?"

This question obviously has a deeper meaning than God desiring to know Adam's geographical location. God knew where Adam was located. God asked this question to alert Adam to his spiritual location. As previously mentioned, Adam was called to stand guard on the horizon between the external world and the garden and to protect the garden from the enemy. This was the location, or post, that the man was mandated to maintain.

If this hierarchal order of sacrificial responsibility is not a prejudice against the woman's dignity, how can we understand it as upholding and elevating the woman?

The Pinnacle of Creation

According to St. Thomas Aquinas, that which is last in execution is first in God's intention.[72] We see this dynamic displayed powerfully in the ancient creation account. As the genesis of

---

71   See Gn 3:9.
72   St. Thomas Aquinas, *Summa Theologica*, II–II, Q. 123, Art. 7.

man unfolds, the complexity of creatures made by God escalates in rational and spiritual complexity.

During the first three days of creation, God established the framework in which all of creation would eventually dwell. On the first day, light is separated from darkness; on the second day, the firmament is separated from the waters; and on the third day, the earth is formed.

During the following three days of the creation account, God populates the pre-existing framework. On the fourth day, God fills the earth with plants, herbs, and vegetation; on the fifth day, God fills the firmament with the celestial beings, the sun, the moon, and the stars; and on the sixth day, God creates beings that move upon the earth such as insects, birds, and animals. Finally, God creates the only creature that is made in His image and likeness,[73] granting him dominion over all of creation.[74]

Man is distinguished from the rest of creation by his being made in the divine image and likeness. As a being comprised of both body and soul, he innately desires the more profound, the spiritual. All that was created prior to man is created for the man, to be subject to the man. Man is the pinnacle of the created

---

73 See Gn 1:26.
74 See Gn 1:28.

order. Yet, there is one who will be created after Adam, and, in a qualified sense, for Adam.

Though from a biological perspective, both men and women are homo sapiens, i.e., they are the same species, even among the genus of humans there exists a hierarchal creative distinction among its species. The woman is created last, which indicates, according to St. Thomas Aquinas, that she is first in God's intention. Woman is the pinnacle of creation. She embodies beauty, fruitfulness, and the perpetuation of the life cycle.

Woman alone is capable of nurturing and forming another life within her and giving birth to one who is created in the image and likeness of God. Though, initially this cannot be accomplished without the man (except for the instance of Christ's conception), the woman alone is life-bearer, as the name Eve signifies.[75] Woman has been endowed with a matriarchal, life-bearing hierarchy that the man does not possess.

With this understanding of woman in mind, we can comprehend more clearly why the man is responsible to God for the woman and her unique ability to form, bear, and nurture life. The man has been given the noble duty to ensure that the pinnacle of created beauty stands untouched and unstained by the devil.

---

75 Hebrew חַוָּה chavah/Havah—chavah, to breathe, and chayah, to live or to give life.

Indeed, by protecting woman, the man not only defends her but also the perpetuation of the image and likeness of God in the child.

A man who desires to protect his treasure does not place it in full view before a thief, but rather hides it, in a sense behind him, so as to keep himself between the thief and his treasure. When a wolf attempts to steal a sheep from the fold, the shepherd does not place the sheep between himself and the predator, but rather stands between the predator and his sheep.

In a similar way, a man does not place the pinnacle of creation, woman, in the position of defending herself from the evils of the world, while idly standing by. The true man stands in the breech between the woman and the world, between her sacred mystery and the secular.

The fact that man is responsible to God for the woman does not deny the woman's dignity or her personal responsibility to God, but rather elevates the dignity of the woman though the man's self-denial.

The glory and wisdom of man being responsible to God for the woman is ultimately understood properly in light of St. Paul's words:

> Let women be subject to their husbands, as to the Lord: Because the husband is head of the wife, as

Christ is head of the church. He is the savior of his body. Therefore, as the church is subject to Christ, so let the wives be to their husbands in all things. Husbands love your wives, as Christ also loved the church, and delivered Himself up for it. . . . So also, ought men to love their wives as their own bodies. He that loves his wife, loves himself. (Ephesians 5:22–25, 28)

According to the holy Apostle, love is synonymous with sacrifice, and headship is synonymous with being a savior; and a savior delivers himself up in sacrifice for his wife.

One sacrifices himself for that which he loves, and, by doing so, he learns to embrace sacrifice. By sacrificing himself for the woman the man attests to the fact that he esteems her as he esteems himself, or as having greater value than himself. A woman strives to submit "in all things" (Eph 5:24) to a man who strives to submit all things to God. This is an aspect of the masculine genius: man has been endowed with a *hierarchal sacrificial responsibility*, and this sacrificial responsibility complements woman's matriarchal mystery.

My brother, be assured of this: there is perhaps no greater, more noble calling that so closely emulates Christ, than this sacred responsibility.

The Role and Responsibility of St. Joseph

An unfortunate prevailing attitude in the minds of some members of the Church living amidst the modern world is the disdain for, or an outright denial of, male headship. Unfortunately, there is a prevalence among many modern fathers of the Church to avoid discussing male headship, or an unwillingness to give men a vision of Christian manhood. By neglecting headship, they deny their own priestly fatherhood. A significant number of modern Church theologians are often ashamed of fatherhood and therefore, perhaps without being aware of it, are ashamed of God's fatherhood, for that is the image they bear.

The popular argument used to resist male headship is that patriarchy (father leadership) is an antiquated, Old Testament, cultural norm from which the Church of the New Testament has graduated and has been liberated. They support their position by referencing Christ's elevation of women's social status, particularly the Lord's Blessed Mother.

Though woman has indeed been liberated from the social impediments that in certain cultures and global regions suppressed her dignity and honor; nevertheless, this liberation of the true woman does not release her from living in proper relationship to the man. If a woman be true, she does not deny or reject the true mission of her husband, but rather supports such sacrifice as exemplified in St. Joseph.

By peering into St. Joseph's marriage to Mary, we will understand more fully why this resistance to male headship is contrary to God's will. Consider for a moment the sublime nature of the Blessed Virgin Mary. The angel Gabriel, during the event of the Annunciation, addressed Mary with the words, "Hail, full of grace" (Lk 1:28).

The Greek translation for the phrase "full of grace" is actually one word, *kecharitomene*, which contains the Greek root word *charitoo* (which means to give grace).

> The word [*kecharitomene*] is the past perfect tense, meaning that the action of giving grace had already occurred. It was not something that was about to happen to her but something that has already been accomplished. The word was also a title. The angel did not say, "Hail Mary, you are *kecharitomene*" but rather, "Hail, *kecharitomene*." Therefore, the word is not simply an action but an identity.[76]

---

76 Fr. Charles Grondin, "'Full of Grace' Versus 'Highly Favored,'" Catholic Answers, www.catholic.com/qa/full-of-grace-versus-highly-favored, accessed on 3/19/2020.

In other words, Mary's identity is that she is full of grace, which God endowed to the Virgin at the moment of her conception. Mary then is the immaculately conceived woman, the new, sinless virgin, and fulfillment of Eve.

In the beginning of humanity's origin, a sinless, virgin woman was created as the mother of creation, and also, at the beginning of the New Testament, a *New Genesis* occurs in which we see a sinless virgin, whose identity is not simply being one who is void of sin but rather, and more importantly, full of grace. She is truly the mother of creation in the order of grace.

What then is first in God's intention is last in execution. God created the Blessed Virgin Mary as the pinnacle of the created order. There exists none, among the human species, of a higher or more glorious rank. She is the one who contained the Word whom the world could not contain.

With these considerations in mind, let us consider the question: How did God communicate His commands for the purpose of directing the Holy Family? Considering that Mary is "full of grace" (Lk 1:28) and that her Son is "full of grace and truth" (Jn 1:14), it would seem most reasonable that divine guidance would be communicated directly to Jesus. However, due to his infancy or young age, Mary the Mother of God would be the optimal receiver of divine direction. Yet, St. Matthew in his Gospel demonstrates emphatically that God communicated his commands to the Holy Family directly to St. Joseph.

To emphasize the perfection of an idea, a Hebrew author would say the same thing in three different ways, for example, "Keeping steadfast love for thousands, forgiving *iniquity*, *transgression* and *sin*" (Ex 34:7, emphasis added). Notice that the Hebrew author emphasizes the perfection of God's forgiveness by describing what he forgives in three different ways.

Similarly, St. Matthew uses this technique in displaying St. Joseph's authority and divinely ordained role to lead the Holy Family by saying it in three ways on three occasions: first, St. Joseph received God's command (while dreaming) to take Mary his wife unto him;[77] second, St. Joseph is commanded to take the child and his Mother and flee to Egypt from Herod;[78] and third, the guardian of the Holy Family is commanded by God to take the child and his Mother to return to the land of Israel.[79]

After Mary's Annunciation, the only communication from God to the Holy Family recorded in the Sacred Scripture prior to our Lord's public ministry is always to St. Joseph. This lends

---

77   See Mt 1:20.
78   See Mt 2:13.
79   See Mt 2:30.

credence to the belief that God endowed St. Joseph with head-ship over the Holy Family.

As with Adam, God selected the man to be the receiver of the divine commands and share these divine commands with the woman—even if that woman was perfect. St. Joseph, though being the least perfect member of the Holy Family, was appoint-ed to be the representative authority of God, and the humble Virgin allowed St. Joseph to lead humbly. This appears to demon-strate that God has ordained the man, the husband, and father as primary in the hierarchal order of sacrificial responsibility.

Bear in mind that God approached the original man first after he had sinned, confirming Adam's responsibility for the garden. Though St. Joseph did not commit a transgression, God approached him, commanding him to "take unto thee Mary thy wife, for that which is conceived in her, is of the Holy Spirit," (Mt 1:20) for the purpose of confirming his role and responsibility to be the guardian of the sacred garden of Mary, and to be *head of the Holy Family*.[80] Indeed, Sacred Scripture confirms this proper male headship repeatedly.[81]

Does this mean that God does not communicate his inspi-rations to the woman, or communicate His presence in a lesser

---

80 See Litany of St. Joseph.
81 See 1 Cor 14:34–35; 1 Pt 3:1; Ti 2:5; Col 3:18; 1 Cor 11:3; Eccl 25:30; Eph 5:23.

way to the woman than the man? By no means. Oftentimes, it is the woman who has far more intense and more numerous spiritual inspirations than the man. However, this does not diminish the fact that the man is responsible for the woman, the child, and the family. Considering these things, we may say in truth that the husband-father is God's primary representative in terms of authority for the domestic church.

Regardless as to how blameless, holy, and wise your wife is, nevertheless, like Adam and St. Joseph, you are called by God to be responsible for her and your children's spiritual well-being.

Indeed, if there is none to lead, none will follow; and if you, my brother, lead not your family from evil, evil will lead your family.

Jesus, the New Adam and His Great Command

By examining our Lord Jesus as the New Adam, in light of his patriarchal predecessors and types, St. Joseph and Adam, we will encounter the most compelling and convincing example of sacrificial responsibility.

The original command given to Adam shortly after God placed him in the garden of paradise and the commands given to St. Joseph regarding Mary, the celestial paradise, culminate and are summed up in the single command that Jesus received from His Father:

> No man taketh [my life] away from Me: but I lay it down of myself, and I have the power to lay it down: and I have the power to take it up again. This commandment have I received of my Father. (John 10:18)

The command that Jesus received from His Father was to lay down His life for His Bride, His spiritual Body, the future Church[82] and, by the power of His Father, to raise Himself from the earth that the Body of the Church may follow Him in the Resurrection.

The man, *Adam,* can be translated as meaning *from the earth.* As with many of the Old Testament patriarchs, their names contained a dual meaning, signaling one's identity and one's destiny.

For example, the name Moses means to draw out from water. Moses was literally drawn out from the Nile River by Pharaoh's daughter, who named him Moses.[83] Although the name identified Moses, the name also hinted at his destiny: God drew Moses and the Israelites through the Red Sea.

The name of the Old Testament patriarch Jacob means he

---

82   See Eph 5; Rev 21.
83   See Ex 2:5.

supplants.[84] Though this was the name that identified Jacob, it also prophetically foretold his destiny. Jacob stole the blessing of the first-born son from Isaac, his father, thus supplanting his older brother Esau.

Returning to the name and meaning of Adam, we discover an indication of his identity, and—though this is not conclusive—perhaps his optimal destiny. Adam's name indicates that he was created "from the earth." Yet the name Adam could hint also at his hoped-for destiny. Can we speculate that if he, as a sinless, virgin man, stood in the breech and protected Eve from being seduced by the serpent, that act of defense may have—hypothetically speaking—cost him his life? God would have raised the sinless Adam from the earth for as Scripture confirms, "Thou will not let your holy one see decay" (Ps 16:10). Yet, Adam died and returned to the dust rather than rising from it.

Our Lord Jesus is the definitive fulfillment of Adam.[85] Jesus

---

84 See Gn 27:36.

85 See Rom 5:12–18; "St. Paul tells us that the human race takes its origin from two men: Adam and Christ. . . . The first man, Adam, he says, became a living soul, the last Adam a life-giving spirit. The first Adam was made by the last Adam, from whom he also received his soul, to give him life. . . . The second Adam stamped his image on the first Adam when he created him. That is why he took on himself the role and the name of the first Adam, in order that he might not lose what he had made in his own image. The first Adam, the last Adam: the first had a beginning, the last knows no end. The last Adam is indeed the first; as he himself says: "I am the first and the last" (St. Peter Chrysologus, *Sermo 117*: PL 52, 520–521." *CCC*, 359.

refused to eat from the Tree of Knowledge of Good and Evil. "Although He was God, He refused to deem equality with God something to be grasped at" (Phil 2:5); rather, He submitted His will to His Father. Though our Lord, being the Second Person of the Trinity, could determine what is good and evil, He rather subjected himself to the authority of God the Father, accepting His Father as His ultimate authority. As the Head of the mystical Body, the Church, Jesus sets the standard—in light of His divine nature—that submission and obedience is most pleasing to and expected by God.

Rather than grasping for the fruit of death from the forbidden tree, Jesus donated the fruit of His mother's womb to the Cross, which has become the Tree of Life. By doing this, Jesus, as the New Adam, fulfilled the command given to the original Adam, while also fulfilling the command given to him by his Father to lay down His life and raise it up again.

Our Lord assumed the prophetic nature of the name Adam and fulfilled the depth of its meaning by *rising from the earth*, definitively defeating sin and death in His Body by means of His Resurrection.

In our Lord Jesus, we discover the ultimate expression and summation of manhood: He refused to eat from the Tree of Knowledge of Good and Evil, but instead donated His life for the Bride that she may be free of its curse. We are often tempted to define what we believe is good for us, rather than humbly submitting to God's commandments. The man who is obedient to God offers Him true sacrifice, for his act of obedience sacrifices his pride and self-importance, thus demonstrating that he is a most trustful and trustworthy son.

As the virginal father, St. Joseph strove to defend Mary and the child Jesus from Herod,[86] so also Christ, in a more definitive way, sacrificed himself to ensure that His Bride, the Church, is safe from "Herod" the devil, who attempts to devour her children.

So also, my brother, to be a true man in the image of Jesus Christ, we must embrace our hierarchal status of sacrificial responsibility. Indeed, your responsibility is to sacrifice your self-importance and vain ambitions for the purpose of protecting and perfecting your wife who is a life-bearer, a figure of the pinnacle of the created order. For if you perfect her in Christ's love, Christ's love will most certainly perfect you.

---

86   See Mt 2:13.

CHAPTER 4

A Husband's Headship

AT THE SERVICE OF COMPLETING THE BRIDE

Unless the grain of wheat falling into the ground die, itself
remaineth alone. But if it die, it bringeth forth much fruit.

—John 12:24–25

The Need for Woman

A man is compromised, if not weakened severely, when he is not complete, and, by his very nature, he is incapable of completing himself. Until he finds one who can complete him, he experiences an unsettling disquiet in his soul that is marked by loneliness. His sensitivity to the experience of loneliness and its grinding ache instinctively heightens a man's internal awareness of his need for another and inspires him to be in relationship with another.

Considering this—humanly speaking—God has designed the woman to encourage and enliven the man to be a person of strength. Indeed, the Hebrew name Eve (ḥaw·wāh) means living, or enlivening, which can signify that her identity is not only to bear another human life, but that she is to be a source of encouragement to the man. The name Eve is derived from the Hebrew verb *hawa*, which means to help another to live collectively.[87] Woman has a particular ability to help the man live in communion with her and also, in a more universal sense, with others. Yet, very often woman can bring out man's deep-seated, subjective, weakness. Without woman, man experiences the pain of loneliness, but with her he endures the fire of purification.

There is a significant correlation between a man who has a healthy, supportive relationship with his wife and his level of spiritual strength. Relationships that help complete the other—though they are incapable of completely fulfilling the other—foster the process of purification from selfishness. This purification, which is a product of the marital relationship, can result in a fulfillment that neither of the two people entering into the relationship possesses in themselves.

---

87   Eve. Abarim Publications, www.abarim-publications.com/Meaning/Eve.html#
anc-1, accessed on 3/19/2020.

We must be clear that no woman can fulfill a man, nor can any man fulfill a woman. Though the two, in a certain sense, are designed to help complete the other, they can never completely fulfill the other.

The endeavor of the two striving to become one subjects the couple to the only One who can help them become complete, fulfilled, and truly happy.[88] The two together, by means of their need for the other and their inability to always please the other, lead one another to the only One who can help them please one another.[89]

By means of the two entering into relationship with one another, they are required to deny themselves for the sake of the other. Paradoxically, the self-denial necessary for a relationship to thrive is a painful, purgatorial fire that eventually leads one to happiness.[90]

God ordained that the greatest hope for society is always discovered by means of sacrificial love, particularly between

---

88 "The Beatitudes respond to the natural desire for happiness. This desire is of divine origin: God has placed it in the human heart in order to draw man to the One who *alone* can fulfill it." *CCC*, 1718, emphasis added.

89 "Willed by God in the very act of creation (cf. Gn 1–2), marriage and the family are interiorly ordained to fulfillment in Christ" (cf. Eph 5). *FC*, 3.

90 Our Lord said, "Amen, amen, I say to you, unless the grain of wheat falling into the ground die, Itself remaineth alone. But if it die it bringeth forth much fruit" (Jn 12: 24–25). Our Lord tells us that if a person, represented by the grain of wheat, does not die to himself for the sake of others, in the end such a man will be alone, which according to God is bad. However, if a man dies to himself, his selfish, inordinate attachments for the sake of service to God and his neighbor, he will in the end achieve a rich communion between himself and God, and himself and his neighbor.

men and women.[91] The history of humanity, comprised of billions of relationships and marriages between a man and a woman bears witness to these truths.

As a couple ages and compiles years upon years of experiential self-denial and sacrifice for the other, while remaining faithful to the other, their love for one another increases. Simultaneously, they individually decrease; that is, they die to selfishness. Yet this "love is stronger than death"[92] and fosters fulfillment in God who created it. Therefore, in relationship to his wife, a man is to live by the example and words of St. John the Baptist, "He must increase, but I must decrease." (Jn 3:30). Indeed, when a husband deliberately sacrifices his selfishness for his wife's betterment, God within her increases, thus elevating the two and their marriage to glorified proportions of seamless unity.

A woman, therefore, can help a man become a true man; yet a woman cannot make him a true man. This is crucial to understanding and living in proper relationship to the woman: only God can make a man into a true man. Nevertheless, God

---

91 "God is love (1 Jn 4:8) and in Himself He lives a mystery of personal loving communion (cf. *GS*, 12). Creating the human race in His own image and continually keeping it in being, God inscribed in the humanity of man and woman the vocation, and thus the capacity and responsibility, of love and communion. Love is therefore the fundamental and innate vocation of every human being." *FC*, 11.

92 See Sg 8:6.

chooses, in His divine wisdom, to do so by means of the man living in relationship with the woman.

Masculinity finds its fulfillment in spiritual paternity, and the pinnacle of manhood is spiritual fatherhood. Manhood is not a destination, but rather a stage of transition to spiritual fatherhood. Without spiritual fatherhood, the world languishes, if not devolves.[93]

The spiritual father moves beyond caring for himself only and intentionally cares for his wife, and eventually the children she bears, even at the cost of himself. Because of these vocational cares, the spiritual father senses his duty to make the world a better place for his family and also other families. Because of this, a man's vocational responsibilities, if embraced, can lead to his redemption.[94]

God has designed woman and the institution of marriage to move a man through the stages of boyhood, manhood, and

---

93 "Above all where social and cultural conditions so easily encourage a father to be less concerned with his family or at any rate less involved in the work of education, efforts must be made to restore socially the conviction that the place and task of the father in and for the family is of unique and irreplaceable importance (John Paul II, Homily to the Faithful of Terni [March 19, 1981], 3–5: AAS 73 [1981], 268–271). As experience teaches, the absence of a father causes psychological and moral imbalance and notable difficulties in family relationships." FC, 25.

94 "If it is true that marriage may also be a *remedium concupisentiae* (see St. Paul: "It is better to marry than to burn"—1 Co 7:9) then this must be understood in the integral sense given it by the Christian Scriptures, which also teach of the "redemption of the body" (Rom 8:23) and point to the sacrament of matrimony as a way of realizing this redemption." *Person and Community: Selected Essays, Karol Wojtyla's,* 327.

ultimately to spiritual fatherhood. Without the woman, it is gravely difficult for a man to become who he is designed to be: a father in the image of God the Father.[95]

Many men are confused regarding this point. Often a man intuits that by being in relationship with a woman he unlocks his masculine genius—which is correct. Yet, a man is often duped into believing that a woman is *the source and summit* of his manhood; yet, as St. Thomas says, "God alone satisfies."[96]

When a man clings to a woman as the source of his identity, he becomes weak, pusillanimous, and domesticated. He inadvertently misunderstands his unique and unrepeatable role as being from God and for God, and, by doing so, he neglects his responsibility to God for his wife and children. Rather than the woman helping link the man to God, she becomes an obstacle to his achieving union with God. Thus, the woman who was created by God to help the man become one with God becomes a type of idol. He esteems her as having greater importance than God.

If he remains in this dynamic, he will live in continual fear of displeasing her, and, being enslaved to her, he will displease

---

95 "Christian revelation recognizes two specific ways of realizing the vocation of the human person in its entirety, to love: marriage and virginity or celibacy. Either one is, in its own proper form, an actuation of the most profound truth of man, of his being 'created in the image of God.'" *FC*, 11, emphasis added.

96 St. Thomas Aquinas, Expos. in symb. apost. I.

the Lord. Rather than being an icon of the Lord's love for him, she becomes his idol. Fearful of losing her, his true identity is lost, and therefore he fails to lead his wife and family to their divine destiny. In a word, rather than exercising relentless trust in God, he is bound by self-doubt. This personal doubt convinces him to cling to her, hoping that she will give him the confidence that he lacks.

On the other hand, there exists a tendency in man to believe that woman is not necessary for his salvation. Such a man believes that he is "above" the woman and will only lower himself to her when he can use her for his own disordered gratification. Yet, it was God who is said "it is not good for man to be alone" (Gn 2:18).There is also a tendency among some men to avoid being in a relationship with a woman altogether for fear of rejection or failure. However, it is precisely by enduring and overcoming such feminine rejection—even if it is a repeated occurrence—that the man will eventually find his strength in the Lord.

Let us return once again to the original Adam to gain greater insight into these matters. By understanding God's original plan for both Adam and Eve and comparing them to the virginal couple of the *New Genesis*, Mary and Joseph, we will see more clearly Christ's relationship with His Bride, the Church, while also comprehending more profoundly why our wives are essential in helping us become heroic, valiant, sacrificial men of God, and how a husband's headship is at the service of completing his bride.

Adam's Solitude

Shortly after God placed the man in the garden, and after giving him the *definitive command*,[97] the author of Genesis recounts the words of God as if the Lord God was thinking to Himself, "It is not good for man to be alone: let us make him a help like unto himself" (Gn 2:18).

From these succinct words we can derive three insights: first, that loneliness is not good and not from God. Second, man's need for woman is essential to the divine plan (therefore, it is not good that man be alone). Third, the divine purpose of marriage is, in a certain sense, revealed through a hint of God's self-disclosure, which aids us, who are created in His image, to understand how to live and love.

In this passage, the Hebrew word for alone, *abadad*, literally means bad. From the divine perspective, it is *bad* that the man is alone, without a partner like himself.

---

97   See Gn 2:17.

The sacred writer communicates this truth in the same breath as "let *us* make him a help like unto himself" (Gn 2:18, emphasis added). Indeed, there is a profound association between God's identity as "us" and man's need for a helper who will complement and help complete him, making the couple a human "us" in the image of God.

God, speaking of himself, grants a clue to his identity with the words "let us" (Gn 1:26), which, for a monotheistic Jewish believer, proposes a theological quandary. How can God speak in plurality regarding His singular divine nature?

From the very beginning, without being explicit, God hints at His Triune identity. This coupled with the fact that God said, "Let *us* make man to *our* image and likeness" (Gn 1:26, emphasis added), earlier in the Genesis account reveals that man images God, who is Relationship, when man lives in relationship with another.[98] Therefore, marriage has been created to draw man and woman into the uncreated relationship of the Trinity.

It is therefore "bad" for the man to be alone. By living in isolation, a man fails to learn how to love like God who is eternal, mutual, self-giving love. By living in relationship with woman, a man learns to live in relationship with God.

---

98 "Man becomes the image of God not so much in the moment of solitude as in the moment of communion." John Paul II, General Audience (November 14, 1979).

To be clear, this does not exclude the celibate or the priest who has intentionally abstained from marriage as a personal sacrifice to God.[99] The example of Jesus Christ demonstrates that a priest—even Christ Himself, the great High Priest[100]—lives in relationship with the "Bride," His Church.[101] Therefore, a priest or celibate can discover his fatherhood by participating in the analogy of the marriage of Christ and the Church.

Though Christ did not need anyone to help Him redeem the world, He nevertheless would not redeem the world without Mary. The Blessed Virgin is a pinnacle symbol of the Bride, Christ's Church (the woman foreshadowed in Genesis 3:15), who participated in the act of redemption by means of her "birth pangs" at the foot of the Cross.[102]

---

99 "Though it is possible to conceive man as solitary before God, however, God Himself draws him from this 'solitude' when He [creates] 'a helper fit for him.' Thus, the continent person "is capable of discovering in his solitude . . . a new and even fuller form of intersubjective communion with others." John Paul II, General Audience, Celibacy for the Kingdom (May 5, 1982).

100 See Heb 4:14.

101 See Eph 5 regarding the marital analogy of Christ and His Church.

102 "Therefore, we know that by the merits of her *dolors* she cooperated in our birth to the life of grace; and hence we are the children of her sorrows. 'Christ,' says Lanspergius, 'was pleased that she, the cooperatress in our redemption, and whom he had determined to give us for our Mother, should be there present; for it was at the foot of the cross that she was to bring us, her children forth.'" St. Alphonsus de Liguori, *The Glories of Mary*, 642; And, "The cross and nails of the Son were also those of his Mother; with Christ crucified the Mother was also crucified." St. Augustine as quoted by St. Alphonsus de Liguori, *The Glories of Mary*, 642.

If our Lord deemed *the woman* to be his collaborator in the redemption of mankind, we must also conclude that living in a relationship with woman, both literally and spiritually, is fundamental to man's meaning, and also your meaning as a man.

Which raises the question: Why is this important? My brother, you will be tempted often, if not continually, to view your wife as a hindrance to your hopes, aspirations, and endeavors. From the world's perspective, such an idea is expressed by thoughts like "she's holding you back" become extremely persuasive. Yet, from the divine perspective, to flee from living in relationship with your wife, and not to love her as Christ loves the Church, is a greater hindrance to your true mission and to your salvation.

The Holy Desire

Shortly after stating that it is not good for the man to be alone, God then proceeds to bring the beasts and fowls that He created to Adam that he may name them. But for Adam there was not found a helper like unto himself.[103]

> [The man] might have reached the conclusion, on the basis of the experience of his own body, that he

---

103 See Gn 2:18.

was substantially similar to the other living beings (*animalia*). But, on the contrary . . . he reached the conviction that he was alone.[104]

Adam's experience of loneliness indicates that the human person is not fully realized without the complementarity of both sexes.[105] We will realize, through Adam's original experience, that it is not the woman who fulfills him, but rather, by participating in a relationship of mutual self-giving with her, he is trained, prepared, and educated in the school of love and is made capable of living in the relationship of God, who alone satisfies the human desire for happiness.

God's action of bringing the beasts to Adam is not only the sacred writer's way of indicating that God has given the man dominion over creation, but is also his way of indicating that God was awakening the man's holy desire for a suitable partner.[106] In a

---

104 *Theology of the Body*, 39.
105 "Man and woman were made 'for each other'—not that God left them half-made and incomplete: he created them to be a communion of persons, in which each can be 'helpmate' to the other, for they are equal as persons ('bone of my bones . . .') and complementary as masculine and feminine. In marriage God unites them in such a way that, by forming 'one flesh' (Gn 2:24), they can transmit human life: 'Be fruitful and multiply, and fill the earth' (Gn 1:28). By transmitting human life to their descendants, man and woman as spouses and parents cooperate in a unique way in the Creator's work" (cf. GS, 50 § 1). *CCC*, 372.
106 See St. John Chrysostom; Fr. Healy, *The Glories of St. Joseph* (Charlotte, North Carolina: TAN Books, 2013), 371.

sense, God plants this holy desire in Adam's heart that it may be fulfilled by God Himself. Thus, Adam's holy desire for a human partner awakens his desire for the divine partner. When Adam's authentic desire for woman is fulfilled, he intuited that God loved him, which awakened within him a desire to love God in return.

Adam desired a helper, in Hebrew *ezer (help) kenegdo (opposite to him, corresponding to him)*, which can be interpreted as an *essential counterpart, a completion of self.* The man and woman are equal in dignity, but opposite (complementary) to the other.[107]

This indicates that woman is a gift from God and can never be reduced to being an object or a prize that can be won, purchased, or owned. She is man's equal, his partner, and must be valued as such.[108]

The unique gift of woman is that she is a counterpart, another self, a completion of man. She may be created from the man

---

107 The phrase "help meet for him" translates the Hebrew words *ezer kenegdo.* These words are a little difficult for me to translate. *Ezer* literally means, 'help' and is similar in meaning to the English word 'help.' However, *kenegdo*, translated 'meet for him,' is more difficult to translate. The root word, *neged*, literally means 'opposite,' 'in the presence of,' 'over against,' 'in front of', 'corresponding to,' or 'aside.' Literally, *kenegdo* means, 'opposite as to him' or 'corresponding as to him.' The sense of the phrase *ezer kenegdo* is 'an equal but opposite helper to him.' For example, my left hand is the *ezer kenegdo* to my right hand; both hands look alike except they are exactly opposite. Both hands are equal but opposite." "The Family Under Siege: The Role of Men and Women," Ricks College Education Week Presentation (June 7, 2001).

108 "The matrimonial union requires respect for and a perfecting of the true personal subjectivity of both of them. *The woman cannot become the "object" of; domination; and male 'possession.'" MD*, 10.

and in a certain sense for the man, but, ultimately, she is created by God and for God, and the man must ensure that she is God's own, for this is his responsibility.[109]

By living in relationship with his wife, a man becomes capable of holiness, sanctity, and fulfillment. This is true even if a man's wife is a cause of consternation, suffering, and bitterness. How can this be? When a wife is an undeniable cause of difficulties and tensions, she can become a precious treasure to the man in that she can become a means by which he will be purified of selfishness and perfected in disinterested love. When this occurs, the husband images Christ as much as, if not more than, he who lives in peace with his wife. To paraphrase St. Paul speaking of this reality, "God loved us even when we were sinners."[110] When a man loves his wife who appears to be unlovable, his love is likened to that of Christ's love for sinners. As St. John of the Cross said, "Where there is no love, put love and you will find love."

Optimally, however, when the man and woman work together, striving toward a common union through mutual self-donation,

---

109 "Of all visible creatures only man is 'able to know and love his creator' (GS, 12 § 3). He is "the only creature on earth that God has willed for its own sake" (GS, 24 § 3), and he alone is called to share, by knowledge and love, in God's own life. It was for this end that he was created, and this is the fundamental reason for his dignity." *CCC*, 356.

110 "But God commendeth his charity towards us; because when as yet we were sinners." Rom 5:8.

God is glorified by the couple, and the couple is glorified by God.

Considering these reasons, we understand more clearly why God willed that the man be given a suitable partner. Yet, by probing into the account of the creation of woman, we will mine further insights regarding our identity, meaning, and mission as men of God.

> Then the Lord God cast a deep sleep upon Adam: and when he was fast asleep, He took one of his ribs, and filled up flesh for it. And the Lord God built the rib which he took from Adam into a woman: and brought her to Adam. (Genesis 2:21–22)

> This sleep is *a kind of death*; it is as if God suspended the life He gave man, in order to re-shape him that he can begin to live again in another way—being two— man and woman are no longer alone.[111]

Indeed, the Hebrew word for sleep, *tardemah*, signifies a mysterious, supernatural slumber induced by God that placed

---

111 *Navarre Bible*, Commentary on Genesis Chapter 2:21 (City, State: Publishing Company, Year), 49; Hereafter *Navarre Bible*.

Adam in ecstasy. The Greek word for ecstasy, *ekstasis*, literally means to stand outside oneself.

While Adam undergoes a supernatural slumber, God removes one of his ribs and forms the woman from it. Upon waking and seeing the woman, Adam exclaimed, "This is bone of my bones, and flesh of my flesh; she shall be called woman" (Gn 2:23). Adam's ecstasy (being outside of oneself) carries over from his sleep into waking reality as he sees himself in Eve.

This marks a new beginning, "a new way of living,"[112] for Adam in that he is no longer alone. The rib also signifies that the man and woman are of equal dignity. Eve was not created from Adam's lower body to signify that he is to rule over her, nor was she created from his head as if to indicate that she is to rule over him. Eve was created from Adam's side to communicate that the two may be equal in dignity, *but not the same*, while always being subject to one another.[113]

---

112 Ibid, *Navarre Bible*, Commentary on Genesis Chapter 2:21 (City, State: Publishing Company, Year), 49.

113 The fact that the first Genesis creation account speaks of the first man as *ha 'adam* prior to the creation of the woman and then afterward man as *ish* and woman as *ishshah*, coupled with woman being an *ezer kenegdo*, meaning a complementary opposite that forms a whole, along with the figurative language regarding the rib taken from man's side, are multiple ways that the sacred writers of Genesis proclaim the equal dignity and honor of man and woman.

Not only is the man "completed" by the woman, but he also, by receiving her from God, receives his vocational mission. In a sense, Adam consecrated himself (charitably) to Eve, setting himself apart from the realm of the beasts for her that she may also be consecrated to God. From this point on, the man is responsible for keeping the woman's garden.

The Completion of Man's Humanity

Recall, my brother, that when God created the original man, the first thing that his eyes beheld was the uncharted, undiscovered wilderness. The first woman's experience was different. When Eve is brought to life, she has no previous knowledge of a world that exists without a partner, nor the knowledge of that absence.

Eve's initial gaze rests only on Adam, and she receives his response to seeing her. Indeed, her first moment is one of elation as she sees the man rejoicing in her.

It appears that the author of the second creation account is expressing that the woman is instinctively made for relationship, and that an aspect of her feminine genius is her ability to live and be adept socially. Adam's view of the world is that chaos is to be ordered, and his instinct is to shape creation by having proper dominion over it. Often woman understands and views the world in a more social way. In a sense, she understands the world through the man and living in relationship with the man. The world is not viewed or interpreted by Eve as intimidating, for she, at the moment of her creation, was already under the wing of Adam's protection and love.

Another implicit theme that is confirmed by our subjective experience is that woman has an innate longing for men to rejoice in her beauty in the manner that Adam rejoiced in Eve.[114] This need for her man to "see her" is a foundational motivating factor for much of her decisions. Woman longs to be affirmed by man, particularly for her beauty.

Unfortunately, this glorious truth is associated with a dual sadness. Feminine beauty's first sadness comes when a husband ceases to rejoice in his wife's beauty. Time and age weary, erode, and diminish her glorious feminine luster, and because of this the man can often become dissatisfied with his wife and therefore wrongly begin to gaze elsewhere. When she realizes that her husband is no longer edified or rejoices in her beauty, her hope for real love and to be significant to her husband is gradually suffocated, and her interior spirit begins to languish.

---

114 See Gn 2:23.

It is your duty, my brother, to re-engage your wife and pray for the grace to "see her" again, to see her true person in and through her body, which has been so wounded, stretched, and scarred by the stress of sacrificing for you and your children. It is a man's responsibility to affirm his wife's sacrificial beauty.[115]

The second sadness regarding woman's beauty is found in the perpetually repeated cycle of initial joy falling into self-disdain. The woman experiences delight when the man delights in her, but also incredible distress and self-hatred when his gaze leaves her never to return.

Eventually she rises from the shame of rejection and musters enough courage to re-enter the arena of men, looking for one who will rejoice in and affirm her beauty. Her heart is lifted in hope when she finds another man who appears to appreciate her . . . until she is abandoned again.[116] Her heart reflects the words of the bride in the Song of Songs:

---

115 "It is the woman who 'pays' directly for this shared generation, which literally absorbs the energies of her body and soul. It is therefore necessary that *the man be fully aware that in their shared parenthood he owes a special debt to the woman.* No programme of 'equal rights' between women and men is valid unless it takes this fact fully into account." *MD*, 10.

116 This dynamic is confirmed in St. John's Gospel account of the Samaritan woman, who had five husbands, and was living with a sixth man in her attempts to find one who could fulfill her longing for love. Only by meeting Christ, the seventh man, the perfect God-man, is she fulfilled, which is represented by her leaving her water jar at the well. Indeed, she came to the well thirsting for temporal water, and left with her thirst quenched by the Living Water.

> I am black but beautiful. . . . Do not consider me that I
> am brown, because the sun hath altered my color: the
> sons of my mother have fought against me, they have
> made me the keeper in the vineyards: my vineyard I
> have not kept. (Song of Songs 1:4–5)

She, the woman, is black because she allowed herself to be used by men. Yet, within her is a glorious spark of hope that she is truly beautiful. She, like a slave that works in the fields, who is browned by the sun's heat, has been a slave to the lusts of men. In vain, she searches for solace from the sons of Adam, for one who will truly rejoice in her beauty.

Yet, sons of Eve (the woman's mother) have "fought against her," using her, objectifying her, and abusing her beauty for their selfish gratifications. This is the disorder that is a consequence of the curse inflicted upon Eve: "He shall have dominion over thee" (Gn 3:16).

Rather than sons of Adam being the guardian of her garden, they abandon her to "keep her own," and, without man's protective presence, woman is highly vulnerable. This is one of the keys to interpreting Eve's creation: she was created with the man already being present as her guardian, and, without his chaste, faithful protection, she is left vulnerable to the serpent's seductive temptations. She is left to keep her own vineyard, alone.

What then can we learn from these reflections? Adam awoke from his divinely induced slumber, no longer alone, but with one who "completes" his humanity. In a sense, he finds himself in her. From this moment onward, woman by means of her very presence is a perpetual reminder to the man of his mission.

The woman's spiritual, emotional, physical, and intellectual beauty summons man to move beyond his self-absorbed microcosm, aiding him to become a warrior of self-giving love.

St. Joseph's Need for the Woman

God creates man with an inherent need and desire for woman for the purpose of motivating the man to live in union with her. When the two "complete" one another[117] the couple becomes a living reflection of the ever-living God. This united front between the husband and wife is the very foundation of families who participate in the making of a faithful Church and virtuous, hardworking, moral societies. This united front is the bedrock of civilization without which it crumbles.

---

117 By saying the two complete one another is not implying that somehow the couple is complete, whole, entire and spiritually fulfilled without God. The idea of completeness is derived from the two becoming one flesh. Humanity is only complete when comprised of both sexes in union with one another.

Yet, why would God instill within man a desire for woman, only to have that desire become thwarted by not fulfilling that desire, or removing the desired woman from his life? What good can come from having a desire for a woman, yet not having that desire completely filled?

Some have said that God does not give an authentic desire to man that He does not wish to fulfill.[118] Reality and experience testify that many a man has authentic, sincere desires—particularly for union with a woman—that are never fulfilled. What sense can we make of this?

More important to God than giving man what he wants is giving him what he needs. Often God will instill a desire in a man's heart, while not fulfilling that desire, for the purpose of purifying the man of his attachment to the creature that he may freely love the Creator above all else. If and when he is free to love, he becomes capable of receiving his heart's desire from God without exploiting, objectifying, abusing, or deterring it from God.

---

118 "Jesus, because He is Eternal, regards not the time but only the love . . . for us, and that He would not inspire me with the desires I feel if He were unwilling to fulfill them" (St. Thérèse, *Story of a Soul* (Washington, DC, ICS Publications, 1996); It must be noted that St. Thérèse desired to be a missionary. During her lifetime on earth she was not able to fulfill that desire; however, God granted her desire by inspiring the Church to make her patroness of missionaries. Again, St. Paul desiring to spread the Gospel of Jesus Christ to Asia was denied his desire: "And when they had passed through Phrygia, and the country of Galatia, they were forbidden by the Holy Ghost to preach the word in Asia" (Acts 16:6).

The authentic desire to live in relationship with woman, and perhaps the absence of not having that relationship, is intended to forge the man. Indeed, the desire for woman is the very context for the purification and perfection of the man.

In the beginning, the original man was incomplete without the woman, and, at the "new beginning," St. Joseph, a type of Adam, was convinced that Mary, *the woman*, no longer needed him. God was the Father of Mary's child, and therefore St. Joseph assumed that a human father was unnecessary. Because of his inability to penetrate the mystery of what was occurring in Mary, he was minded to put her away privately.[119]

Within this moment of consternation amidst an unprecedented, perplexing situation—whether it lasted three hours, three weeks, or three months—St. Joseph returned to the ache of Adam's solitude prior to the original man receiving the first woman.

---

119 "Why did Joseph want to leave his spouse, Mary? Listen not to my opinion, but to that of the Fathers. He thought to leave Her for the same reason why Peter kept the Lord at a distance, saying, 'Depart from me, Lord, for I am a sinner' (Lk 5:8), or the Centurion did not want the Lord to come to his house, saying: 'Lord, I am not worthy that you enter my house' (Mt 8:8). Likewise, Joseph, retaining himself to be unworthy and sinful, went away saying that he would not be able to live with a woman who was so great, whose wonderful and superior dignity he feared. He saw and feared the woman who bore a certain sign of the divine presence; and since he was not able to penetrate the meaning of this mystery he wanted to leave Her in a hidden way. Peter was fearful in the face of such power, the Centurion before the majesty of His presence. Also Joseph, as a man, feared the newness of such a great miracle; he was afraid of the profoundness of such mystery; and decided to leave Her in a hidden way." St. Bernard, *Laudes Mariae*, 2, 13–16.

When as [Jesus'] mother Mary was espoused to
Joseph, before they came together, she was found
with child, of the Holy Ghost. Whereupon Joseph her
husband, being a just man, and not willing publicly
to expose her, was minded to put her away privately.
(Matthew 1:18–19)

Before proceeding to discuss the perplexity of St. Joseph's
situation, it is important to note that St. Matthew the Evangelist places tremendous emphasis on clearly stating the fact that
Mary and Joseph, at the time of the event of Mary's Annunciation, were indeed married. So emphatic is he on this point
that the sacred writer states this truth on four occasions in four
varied ways within five verses:

When . . . Mary was *espoused* to Joseph . . . (Mt 1:18)
Whereupon Joseph her *husband* . . . (Mt 1:19)
Joseph, son of David, fear not to take unto thee Mary *thy
wife* . . . (Mt 1:20)
And Joseph rising . . . took unto him *his wife*. (Mt 1:24)

As we have discussed, there are many reasons why St.
Matthew deliberately emphasizes this fact. However, for our

purposes in this chapter, we will use this quadruple emphasis to not only confirm that Mary and Joseph were indeed married, but also to demonstrate that the essence and character of this marriage was virginal.

Mary and Joseph's virginal marriage is the lens through which we become capable of entering the heart of St. Joseph and understanding his reason for putting Mary away privately, which may have been one of the most challenging and heart-rending decisions that St. Joseph had ever made.

Indeed, by understanding his reason for separating himself from Mary, we will discover valuable lessons pertaining to man's ache for a partner, the power and reason for solitude before God, and the effect it can have on every man if he chooses to embrace this dark night.[120]

As we will see, St. Joseph undergoes a series of sequential events similar in character to Adam: a dark night of solitude born from a need for woman, followed by a sleep, followed by man awakening to receive woman and his vocational mission.

Let us, my brother, go to St. Joseph and learn from his example the vital importance of solitude with God, and discover the

---

120 This "dark night" can be due to many causes such as: a wife is distant emotionally from her husband; an infirm wife; a wife unwilling to unite in sexual intercourse; a wife never healing from wounds of the past, even and especially those inflicted by her husband; her divorcing the husband; her infidelity; or her death.

grace that affords man the ability to rise above all attachments and experience the freedom to love freely.

St. Joseph: Releasing the Need to be Needed

Did St. Joseph consider divorcing Mary? By examining the scriptures more attentively, we discover that St. Joseph, most likely, was not considering to divorce our Lady, as much as he was considering to dismiss her from himself. The Greek word for put her away, *apoluo*, means to set free, or to release. While this word could be used in the context of divorce, in this situation, the word is qualified by the Greek word *lathra*, which means secretly.

To divorce Mary demanded that St. Joseph would subject her to a legal procedure that would have "exposed her" to the judgments of men and the Law.[121] Yet, to "set free" and "release" her "privately" indicates a positive action of protection from judgment—a liberation from the marital bond. It appears that this could be the most respectful way that St. Joseph could have dismissed Mary.

Why then did St. Joseph consider liberating Mary secretly from her marriage commitment? We discover a clue in Mary's response to the angel Gabriel's words, "Behold thou shalt

---

121 See Lv 20:10; Nm 5:16–27; Jn 8:4–5.

conceive in thy womb, and shalt bring forth a son; and thou shalt call his name Jesus." (Lk 1:31). During the Annunciation, Mary responded to God's messenger with a question, "How shall this be done, because I know not man?" (Lk 1:34).

Consider that after hearing the divine decree that the Son of God would be conceived in her, Mary would have understood that she was already married (betrothed) to St. Joseph and logically assumed that after the second stage of Jewish marriage, the solemnization, she and St. Joseph would have sexual intercourse and the fruit of that union would be the Son of the Most High.

Yet, Mary did not make this conclusion. Rather, she asked, "How can this be?" indicating that she did not understand how she could conceive, or would conceive, because of a previous commitment of which God was aware. Mary's response is logical only if she had made a vow of virginity to God, and to St. Joseph, previously. If she had not made a vow of virginity to God and St. Joseph, she would have assumed that sexual intercourse with St. Joseph would consequently produce the Son of God. In addition to this, the angel said, "You *shall* conceive" (future tense), but did not indicate how Mary would conceive until the Holy Virgin questioned the divine messenger.

Mary's virginal consecration of herself to God appears to be contrary to dominant beliefs and practices of the Jews who birthed sons in hopes that one of them would be the greatly anticipated Messiah. Mary's vow of virginity, however, reflected more accurately the faith of the Jews who were very familiar with the prophecy from Isaiah: "A virgin shall conceive, and bear a son ..." (Is 7:14).

Let us return to the original question: Why would St. Joseph consider to secretly (*lathra*) liberate or release (*apoluo*) Mary from being married to him?

Based on the aforementioned conclusions it seems highly plausible that St. Joseph, by the time of his betrothal to Mary, was well aware of several things regarding the person of Mary: first, he knew that Mary had made a complete self-offering to God by means of a vow of perpetual virginity. Mary would not have hidden this from St. Joseph, lest their marriage would have not been valid.[122] Second, St. Joseph's love for Mary was so intense that he decided to follow her in this decision of being a chaste, celibate spouse. Third, St. Joseph was fully aware of Mary's internal beauty, purity, holiness, and intense love for God. Fourth, St. Joseph knew that a woman of this holy stature could not commit adultery.

---

122 "Joseph's co-operation is constituted first and foremost by his consent to be the virginal husband of Mary. Again to appeal to St. Thomas [Aquinas], we say that only by means of Joseph's matrimonial consent could that marriage have been brought into existence which was ordained to receive Christ. Only in the supposition of the marriage contract could Joseph agree with our Lady to live virginally within their union." *Joseph and Jesus: A Theological Study of Their Relationship*, 144.

How can we know this? If St. Joseph had believed that Mary had committed adultery, his act of releasing her secretly, rather than subjecting her to the consequences of transgressing the Mosaic Law, would have been a transgression of the Law.

Indeed, according to the mandate of the Mosaic Law, a woman who became pregnant before the second stage of Jewish marriage (the solemnization) was to be tried publicly and executed as a consequence of her infidelity to her husband and to God.[123]

Yet, St. Matthew clearly states that St. Joseph is a "just man" (Mt 1:19). To be just (*sadek* in Hebrew) is to be righteous as expressed by living in accordance to the Law, being innocent of charge, and seeking God above all else.

If St. Joseph believed that Mary had committed adultery, and then released her, his action would have been contrary to being *sadek*, that is, righteous before God, which raises the question: How can St. Joseph's action of dismissing his wife be understood as being righteous according to the Law?

When we consider that Mary and Joseph were married prior to the conception of Jesus; that the essence of their marriage was a virginal pact, a vow of celibacy to God and to one another; and that St. Joseph did not believe that Mary had committed

---

123 See *FN*, 159.

adultery; we see more clearly why he sought to separate himself from his wife, and why this action was most just.

Upon discovering Mary pregnant without his cooperation, St. Joseph:

> Considering himself unworthy to live with such great sanctity, he wished to hide her away, just as Peter said, depart from me, for I am a sinful man, O Lord (Lk 5:8). Hence [Joseph] did not wish to hand over, i.e., to take her to himself, and receive her in marriage, considering himself unworthy.[124]

St. Joseph's just character is threefold: first, Joseph refused to expose the innocent Mary to those tasked with enforcing the Law. The just man could not ignore the real possibility that Mary's pregnancy was of divine origin. Yet, St. Joseph was also aware that he could not satisfy those who enforced the Law by proving Mary's innocence. By attempting to do so, he would have risked her being publicly shamed and eventually executed.

This is important if we are to properly understand St. Joseph and his just character: first, he was just, *sadek* (innocent of charge), because he didn't dare to allow men to make a charge

---

[124] St. Thomas Aquinas, *Commentary on the Gospel of St. Matthew*, Article 117, 118.

against Mary's innocence. True justice toward one's neighbor is to not accuse someone of something until having certain knowledge of the transgression.

Second, St. Joseph believed himself to be unworthy of the mystery occurring within Mary. St. Joseph sought to liberate Mary from the possibility of him exposing her dignity to that—which he believed—was not worthy of her sanctity (himself).

Third, St. Joseph was just because he did not cling to Mary, viewing her as the source and meaning of his life. St. Joseph was willing to release the creature in exchange for loving and obeying the Creator. The just man sought God above all things and in all matters. Regardless of his intense love for Mary, St. Joseph understood her as God's possession, and the child within her as God's Son; and, therefore, he refused to usurp the authority of God by clinging to his marital rights.

By doing these things, St. Joseph released his need to be needed. This idea of detaching oneself from the need to be needed is very difficult for men. By our very nature we are divinely called, if not mandated, to be providers, protectors, and priests of our domestic churches. In performing these responsibilities, we are respected and valued, and derive great significance.

Let us learn from St. Joseph who, though desiring Mary to be his own, resolved to release her to ensure that she would be God's own. Rather than deriving his significance from a creature—regardless as to how great of a creature she was— St. Joseph became a man who could signify the Creator by means of his disinterested love. It is here, within this moment of deciding not to interfere with God's action in Mary, that St. Joseph, in a qualified sense, died to himself, entering the dark night of solitude.

St. Joseph's Return to Solitude

Studying the life of Adam, the original man, and typologically comparing him to the just man, St. Joseph, we discover a sequential pattern of events that is often repeated in the life of men. The sequential pattern begins with: first, a desire for something not yet given; second, a sadness induced by man's desire not being fulfilled; third, solitude before God, wherein man realizes his helplessness and need for God to intervene (or, if he doubts God, he falls to the temptation to take matters into his own hands, attempting to apprehend the object of his desire); fourth, a rest in God wherein he waits patiently for God to act; and fifth, an arising from that rest to receive the gift desired.

Though Adam and St. Joseph experienced these events, each of them corresponded to the gift of woman (the "object" of desire) differently. Adam, as we are well aware, initially rejoiced in the woman, but failed at fulfilling his noble task of defending her, the "garden enclosed," from the serpent and his seductions; whereas St. Joseph corresponded to the grace afforded by God during his dark night of solitude and, because of this special grace, became the just guardian and keeper of Mary, the "fountain sealed."

St. Joseph repeats Adam's sequence of events, yet with a divine purpose. It is as if God predestined St. Joseph to return to Adam's solitude to retrieve and redeem what was lost in the mission of the first man. Indeed, by examining and entering into St. Joseph's solitude, we discover that solitude before God is the key element to corresponding faithfully to the mission of being the keeper of the garden enclosed.

St. Matthew's Gospel recounts the moment of St. Joseph's solitude: "But while he thought on these things, behold an angel of the Lord appeared to him in his sleep" (Mt 1:20). The Greek word used for while he thought, or as he pondered, is *enthyméomai* (from *en*, meaning in a state or condition, and intensifying *thymós*, meaning a passionate response), thus signifying a passionate frame of mind, easily agitated, or quickly moved by strong, provoking impulses.[125]

125 *Entbymeomai*, Bible Hub, online edition, www.biblehub.com/greek/1760.htm, accessed 3/19/2020.

St. Joseph's act of pondering over his personal dilemma was not mere casual consideration, but rather an intense, spirit-rending event. St. Joseph wrestled with himself over this situation. His soul was deeply grieved by the potential loss of Mary—as indicated by the word *enthyméomai*. Indeed, St. Thomas Aquinas indicates that *thumos*, the root word of *enthyméomai*, is the part of the soul that combats those things that attempt to attack a precious good. St. Joseph combated the devil over the precious good of Mary and his marriage to her. From this we can conclude that St. Joseph experienced—in his soul—the reality that it is *abadad* for man to be alone and that his soul was tormented by the idea of separating himself from the Holy Virgin.

Entering the dark night of solitude, St. Joseph experienced, more intensely than Adam, the anguish of not having a suitable partner. It appears that St. Joseph's pain of losing Mary was so severe that he was unable to emit a word in prayer. Indeed, "We know not what we should pray for as we ought; but the Spirit himself asketh for us with unspeakable groanings." (Rom 8:26). No words are prayed by St. Joseph, yet God hears his prayer. Without speaking, in silence, the tormented St. Joseph presents his interior distress to God.

Alone, before God, St. Joseph wrestled to discern God's will, hoping that God would provide an answer that would sweep away his overwhelming sadness. "Deep calleth on deep (Ps 41:8)"and from the depths of St. Joseph's heart he called out to the God who alone can make haste to help him.[126] Indeed, from the silent depths of St. Joseph's soul, he called out to the depths of the silent God who spoke without His voice being heard.

St. Joseph's dream is a kind of death, wherein his attachment to his hopes and vision of the way things could have been are surrendered to the Almighty God.

The words "in my bed by night, I sought him whom my soul loveth: I sought him, and found him not" (Sg 3:1) apply mystically to St. Joseph's situation. On his bed, amidst a deep sleep, while passionately pondering his situation, he entered the dark night of solitude, seeking God, but initially in silence he found Him not.

My brother, if you accept the calling to become a guardian of the garden, you may not find lasting consolation in ease and comfort, as represented by the bed. Man, guided by God, eventually finds the true God amidst the dark night, the unknown, the veiled and difficult future, the desert of the weary soul; for in his personal dark night he becomes dependent upon one greater than himself.[127]

---

126 See Ps 70:1.
127 We see this characterized figuratively by St. John the Baptist, who was literally

How admirable was St. Joseph's response to his sore dilemma. Rather than responding passionately and attempting to control the situation, he surrendered to God. St. Joseph demonstrated that despite the holy character and motivation behind a desire, that desire must always be surrendered to God.

Many a man presses his advantage, forcing his future, attempting to control his fortunes, while making excuses for his rashness, believing that his pursuits and desires are of holy character. How often does one hear a man say: "God told me to . . ." when the god they speak of is their own internal desire? Yet, "the Lord is good to them that hope in him, to the soul that seeketh him" (Lam 3:25).

Wait on the Lord and be not rash in plundering your pursuits. Be not anxious in hope of obtaining what you think should be yours. God often will allow you to endure many severe trials, withholding a certain good, for the purpose of teaching you how to love that which is greater, to love the Giver of the gift more than the gifts themselves.

He who neglects to enter the dark night of solitude when the Lord appears to deny him some good and impatiently grasps for

---

in the desert at the height of his ministry. St. Luke's Gospel says, "Under the high priests Annas and Caiaphas; the word of the Lord was made known unto John, the son of Zachary, in the desert" (Lk 3:2), which is a mystical symbol of the spiritual life. It is in the desert that is amidst the period of spiritual desolation that the Word of God draws nigh to the one who awaits Him.

what God has not yet given may obtain that good only to bring him to ruin.[128] It is indeed a tremendous challenge for men not to weary of God's faithfulness while in the desert of desolation. Yet, we are to

> Count it all joy, when you shall fall into divers temptations; Knowing that the trying of your faith worketh patience. And patience hath a perfect work; that you may be perfect and entire, failing in nothing. (James 1:2–4)

St. Joseph teaches us that the key to solving our personal dilemmas during the seasons of the spiritual night, when we are deprived of spiritual consolation, is to first enter the silence before God and wait patiently for his counsel and direction. Only after receiving divine inspiration should we rise in obedience to fulfill the command that the Lord has given.

Silence before God affords obedience to God; obedience to God inspires one to sacrifice for God who sacrificed Himself for

---

128 See Nm 11:18–20; 31–35; "As yet the flesh was between their teeth, neither had that kind of meat failed: when behold the wrath of the Lord being provoked against the people, struck them with an exceeding great plague. And that place was called, the graves of lust: for there they buried the people that had lusted. And departing from the graves of lust, they came unto Haseroth, and abode there" (Nm 11:33–35).

all; and sacrifice for God glorifies God, who will in turn glorify the man of sacrifice.[129]

Indeed, St. Joseph's prayer was so intense that it carried over into his sleep. The Scripture confirms that as he pondered his situation an angel of the Lord appeared to him in his sleep. During this sleep, St. Joseph received the command, "Joseph, son of David, fear not to take unto thee Mary thy wife, for that which is conceived in her is of the Holy Ghost" (Mt 1:20).

Some may contend that because St. Joseph received divine revelations he had it easier than the typical man who attempts to navigate the unknown future. Rather than St. Joseph having it easy, he—through years of laboring and learning to pray and receiving much grace in prayer—became capable of hearing and receiving divine counsel. In fact, St. Joseph became proficient in the art of waiting upon God in silence, trusting that the God of truth would direct him.

One can only obey the direction he has received, and one most often receives direction (though veiled) in silence. In silence, a man subdues his inclination toward activity, progress,

---

129 "Whereunto also he hath called you by our gospel, unto the purchasing of the glory of our Lord Jesus Christ" (2 Thes 2:14). St. Paul states that we become co-heirs with Christ, that is inherit His glory, when we suffer with Him: "And if sons, heirs also; heirs indeed of God, and joint heirs with Christ: yet so, if we suffer with him, that we may be also glorified with him" (Rom 8:17).

and initiation, and by doing so he becomes more capable of receiving divine counsel.

> To obey (from the Latin *ob-audire*, to "hear or listen to") in faith is to submit freely to the word that has been heard, because its truth is guaranteed by God. (*CCC*, 144)

St. Joseph, waiting in silence, was assured by God that he was not to separate himself from the Holy Virgin. Indeed, the divine counsel afforded to St. Joseph while sleeping is expressed fittingly by the psalmist, "I will bless the Lord, who hath given me understanding moreover my reins also have corrected me even till night" (Ps 15:7).

The marked difference between the common man and the saint is that the saint discerns what his master desires by entering the silence and waiting for His divine direction. By waiting in silence, he learns to be obedient to his Lord in all things. Through years of painful purification, the saint learns that obedience is better than sacrifice for obedience is the sacrifice of one's pride.[130]

---

130 See 1 Sm 15:22.

For the man of God, prayer is never an afterthought, or the last hope, but rather is the source, the *anima*, the soul of the apostolate. Without days marked by silence in prayer, regardless of how effective we may appear, we achieve very little from the divine perspective, and may actually hinder those around us.[131]

My brother, your interior life gives your exterior life form. Your interior character determines your exterior actions. To give God you must have God. To infuse others with God you must be infused by God. The infusion occurs in prayer—in silence.

The Need for St. Joseph

A reoccurring theme in the spiritual life is to give up something in a spirit of authentic abandonment to God, while maintaining faith in His generosity, only for Him to return the offering in a multiplied, transformed version. The life of Job, Jesus' multiplication of the loaves and fishes donated by a young boy,

---

131 "Let those, then, who are singularly active, who think they can win the world with their preaching and exterior works, observe here that they would profit the Church and please God much more, not to mention the good example they would give, were they to spend at least half of this time with God in prayer. . . .They would then certainly accomplish more, and with less labor, by one work than they otherwise would by a thousand. For through their prayer they would merit this result, and themselves be spiritually strengthened. Without prayer they would do a great deal of hammering but accomplish little, and sometimes nothing, and even at times cause harm." *St. John of the Cross*, Spiritual Canticle, 29, 3.

and Christ's transformation of water into wine at His mother's bidding at the Wedding at Cana of Galilee are all prime examples of this dynamic.

Often, as men, we desire to be important, worthy of attention, and needed by others. In a word, we desire significance. Yet, quite often, God will either remove, or ask us to remove, that which gives us worldly or creaturely significance without the promise, or perceived hope, of receiving anything in return.

The sacrifice of significance in exchange for nothing other than doing the will of God constitutes a "season of night," a spiritual darkness wherein there is very little, if any, spiritual consolation provided by God. It is this night that forges a man. Indeed, this season of night is a purifying fire that burns off all dependence upon significance derived from creatures and leaves the man with the pure, unalloyed desire to signify God alone. This spirituality is expressed forcefully by our Lord Jesus, "I cannot of myself do anything. As I hear, so I judge: and my judgment is just; because I seek not my own will, but the will of him who sent me" (Jn 5:30).

This season of night can be likened to a man who has spent his existence scratching and climbing toward the peak of the mountain of creaturely significance, where he envisions himself planting his flag, a symbol of all of his accomplishments, talents, gifts, and abilities for which the world of creatures will admire him.

As he draws closer to his to his monumental goal, with the peak in sight, the earth begins to quake and suddenly the ground before him gives way, and the final road to the pinnacle of self-glory becomes a vast cavern.

Within his view, the sight of the peak remains, yet the path toward that summit no longer exists. During this moment, the man is confronted with a choice: he can remain set in his place, eyes locked upon his former destiny, attempting to determine ways to build a bridge that can span the chasm to his sought after significance—a project that will cost him all of his resources, including the relationships with those whom he loves—or he can embrace the fact that God has denied him this mountain-top experience and humbly resolve to surrender and enter the ever near cave of silence. This may initially appear to be human weakness, yet such surrender is an act of humility that is dependent upon a greater wisdom than he possesses.

In the cave of silence, the man learns to surrender his pursuits for worldly, creaturely significance and patiently wait upon God to direct his ways. If the silent darkness of the cave is endured, God will replace his disordered desire to be important to creatures with a new desire: to signify the living God. Indeed, significance can be defined as to be worthy of attention or importance.[132]

Yet, to be worthy of another's attention indicates that one derives his worth from those who deem him important or worthy of their attention. In other words, such value is based on what people think of us. This type of significance is finicky, dependent on subjective forces that flicker and fade, wax and wane; they depend upon how the creature assesses us.

Yet, there is a deeper, more profound meaning of the word significance. Significance in Latin, *significare*, is comprised of the two Latin words, *signi* (sign) and *ficare* (to make). In other words, true significance is to be made into a sign that directs humanity to something transcendent and greater than oneself. In the dark cave of silence, God replaces the man's desire to be valued by men with the desire to signify God. Indeed, with Christ he can proclaim, "I receive glory not from men" (Jn 5:41).

With this theme of significance in mind, we return to St. Joseph, who, while having the grand spectacle of marriage to Mary in full view, witnessed his path to her appear to crumble. Rather than clinging to Mary for significance, St. Joseph entered the dark night of silence, surrendering this deep personal desire to God.

---

132 Significance. In Merriam-Webster's online dictionary. Retrieved from http://www.merriam-webster.com/dictionary/significance, accessed 3/19/2020.

It is within this silence that God replaced St. Joseph's desire to be significant to Mary with the unchanging, unfading desire to signify God the Father. God replaces that which is transitive with that which is transcendent, and that which is passing with that which will not fade. Indeed, as with Job, the Lord takes away only to give more abundantly. St. Joseph's life is fitting testimony to this truth. By surrendering his marriage to Mary, St. Joseph eventually became a human icon of God the Father to God the Son.

> Joseph rising up from sleep, did as the angel of the Lord had commanded him, and took unto him his wife. (Matthew 1:24)

After, and only after, St. Joseph endured the night season of detachment from creaturely significance did God grant him something greater. In place of a virginal marriage that would produce no offspring, St. Joseph was given his virgin wife *and* the vocation to be a spiritual father to God the Son. Indeed, St. Joseph surrendered his desires, only to receive the fulfillment of those desires in a multiplied, transformed version for God "is able to do all things more abundantly than we desire or understand, according to the power that worketh in us" (Eph 3:20).

My brother, as Eve complemented and, in a certain qualified human sense, completed Adam, so also St. Joseph—as a type of Adam—rose from sleep to receive the New Eve, Mary, as his own. Mary and Joseph, a New Eve and a New Adam, complement and, humanly speaking, complete each other. Mary expressed her feminine, fully dilated, receptivity before God: "Be it done" (Lk 1:38), whereas St. Joseph expressed his masculine, initiating character of sacrifice by "doing"; indeed, he "did as the angel of the Lord had commanded him" (Mt 1:24).

The same Spirit that hovered over Mary, conceiving the child Jesus in her womb, inspired the sleep of St. Joseph. God removed the rib from Adam to form Eve, and in a similar way—but in reverse—God communicated the same Holy Spirit, who conceived divine life in Mary, to St. Joseph, granting him a new vitality, a new way of living.

> "Joseph did as the angel of the Lord commanded him; he took his wife" into his home (Mt 1:24); what was conceived in Mary was "of the Holy Spirit." From expressions such as these are we not to suppose that his love as a man was also given new birth by the Holy Spirit? Are we not to think that the love of God which has been poured forth into the human heart through

127

the Holy Spirit (cf. Rom 5:5) molds every human love into perfection? This love of God also molds—in a completely unique way—the love of husband and wife, deepening within it everything that bespeaks an exclusive gift of self, a covenant between persons, and an authentic communion according to the model of the Blessed Trinity." (*Guardian of the Redeemer,* 19)

St. Joseph's obedience to the divine command to take Mary, his wife, enabled him to embrace a deeper significance: He became an icon of God the Father, which allowed the Holy Family to become the archetype and "model of the Blessed Trinity"[133] for all mankind.

Though God in Himself has no need for someone, or something, to complete Him, in a very specific way, He has placed himself in the unique position to "need" St. Joseph. By the Word becoming a child, God the Son, becomes dependent upon a human father for protection, provision, and leadership. In a certain, qualified sense, God the Father deliberately chose to need St. Joseph because the Incarnate Son of God needed a human father.

Without St. Joseph, Mary and the Son of God would not

---

133 *GR,* 19.

have survived the requirements of the Law applied to a woman denounced and found guilty of illegitimate relations. Without St. Joseph, the Holy Family would not have become a living reflection of the Trinity's love. Without St. Joseph, the human family would not have attained the full, lived capacity of its identity as an icon of the Trinity.

In a similar way, God the Father "needs" you to be a holy father because your children need God the Father. This is the essential nature of the man who is husband and father.

God relentlessly pursued the just St. Joseph as he pondered his future in the dark night of silence and awakened Joseph to his necessary, vital, and pivotal role as father in the Holy Family. St. Joseph's mission and identity was to "relive and reveal the very fatherhood of God."[134]

My brother, similarly, God is pursuing you, summoning you to become an icon of God the Father to your family, to assume your theological spiritual position as *custos* (guardian) of the garden.

This is the divine paradigm, the expressed truth of the eternal God regarding His Trinitarian character: The Father begets the Son, and from the Father and the Son proceeds the Holy Spirit. The Father, though equal in essence and co-eternal with the Son and the

---

134 See *FC*, 25.

Holy Spirit, begets life. This is proclaimed by St. Thomas Aquinas in his hymn of praise to the Trinity: *"Genitori, Genitoque laus et jubilation, salus, honor, virtus, quoque sit et benediction: procedenti ab utroque compare sit laudation."* The vernacular translation is as follows: "To Begetter and Begotten be praise and jubilation, health, honor, strength also and blessing. To the one Who proceeds from Both be praise as well." The begetter is the Father of the Begotten One. As fatherhood exists in the divine Godhead, so also does fatherhood exist and function in the created order. Fatherhood is the source of life in the family, society and the Church.[135]

St. Joseph's presence as the father of Jesus and the husband of Mary enabled their family to become a living symbol of the Blessed Trinity. In a similar way, by assuming your post, and embracing your vocation to fatherly greatness, your family may become an efficacious witness of the transformative power of God to this fallen world.

Scandal of Our Age

These reflections lead us to discuss one of the greatest scourges and scandals of our age, namely, that among Catholics the divorce rate is very similar to that of the world. Marriage and family have

---

135 Devin Schadt, *The Fathers of St. Joseph Manual: Spirituality and Vision* (Rock Island, Il: The Fathers of St. Joseph, 2015), p 2.

been created by God with the mission to be a living witness of the Gospel, proclaiming that Christ's grace enables us to live a joy-filled life, despite circumstances of tremendous suffering, duress, and tension. Though the Blessed Mother is the immaculately conceived one, and Jesus is the Son of God, St. Joseph was essential to their family becoming a witness to marital fidelity.

The devil's primary targets are marriage and the family. Indeed, fathers and mothers are the key players in God's victory over sin and death, and their children are often the victims of the devil's assaults.[136] He launches his assault with the intention of re-defining the reflected image of the Trinity in the family into a disordered, distorted image that signifies the kingdom of evil, selfishness, fruitlessness, and unbridled lust. It is the devil's intention to divide the family by dividing married couples by removing the man from his divinely ordained position as *custos* (guardian) of the garden.

Yet, "what therefore God hath joined together, let not man put asunder" (Mk 10:9). Divorce then is not an option. Difficulties, tensions, and relational sufferings are not the reason for divorce. Our inability and unwillingness to embrace suffering for the sake of the other is the reason for divorce. Suffering does

---

136 "The last battle will be between God and Satan over the family and marriage." Sr. Lucia.

not prove the need for divorce, but rather testifies to the need for marriages to be a unified whole—and overcome divorce.

In other words, the sufferings, tensions, and battles within marriage are due, in a large part, to its grand calling to cultivate a family in the image of the triune Godhead. Therefore, marriage is the subject of the devil's envy, and it must endure many attacks from the evil one.

My brother, be assured that marriage is a call and path to great sanctity for in no other relationship are two people designated to conform to one another so as to become one flesh, and this is a great mystery in reference to Christ and His Church.[137] This indeed is a great calling.

How often do we as men enter marriage for the purpose of avoiding the suffering of isolation, only to encounter the suffering that, if embraced, eventually produces true communion? We often believe that a good marriage must not endure suffering, yet suffering must be endured, if not embraced, for the good of marriage.

St. Joseph demonstrates to us that, regardless of how unworthy we believe ourselves to be, the call to marriage and raising a family is worthy of man. All men suffer, but few men sacrifice. The sacred summons to be a guardian of the garden demands

---

137 See Eph 5:32.

that you embrace suffering for the sake of your marriage. By doing so, you and your wife will not only complement one another, but help to complete one another, and ultimately attain the fulfillment that God can only offer.

The Supreme Calling of Christ

Christ fully reveals man to himself and makes his supreme calling clear.[138] Only God can reveal to you who you are and who you are to be. Only by reflecting upon Him who is called supreme, may you, as a man, comprehend your supreme calling. We have meditated at length upon man's role and responsibility by peering, in retrospect, into the original man's experience and comparing it with the life of the just man, St. Joseph. Yet, these examples serve the greater purpose of directing us to the God-man, Jesus Christ, who reveals the way to become a man of God.

From the shadowed patriarchal past, images and figures of the true man have emerged in partial and fragmented ways, revealing aspects of man's role and responsibility. By meditating upon the original Adam and St. Joseph, we have discovered a sequential pattern that was revealed and fulfilled definitively in the final Adam, Jesus Christ. It is this pattern that has aided

---

138 See *GS*, 22.

us in our pursuit of discovering man's unique vocation and mission. However, by meditating upon this pattern in the life of Christ, we will see more clearly the vision of man's unique responsibility of spiritual male headship.

Indeed, this headship, ordained and fulfilled by Christ Himself, is the "template" of the supreme calling for every man. This headship, however, particularly in recent history, has come under attack, being vehemently protested by radical feminists and those sympathetic to their position. For the purpose of maintaining equality among the sexes, a husband's headship is rarely mentioned from the Church's pulpits, and its true character and vision has fallen into obscurity.

This "supreme calling" of men, rather than being clearly presented and represented, has become a great source of embarrassment among Church leaders. So concerned are we about offending the world, and worldly women, that we neglect men, and, by neglecting men, we ultimately teach men, though without words, to neglect woman. For if we were to help men become responsible to God for women, men in turn would help women respond to God in union with men.

Now, perhaps more than ever in the history of Christianity, a compelling, honest vision and theology of male headship is not only necessary, but, for the sake of marriage and family, this unique role of man needs to be proclaimed with the utmost humility and without shame or reservation, for by avoiding the discussion of true spiritual headship, we avoid knowing the true Head of the Body. Without knowledge of this Head, we cannot conform to it as His true Body. Ironically, if we deny spiritual male headship within marriage, we may be inadvertently denying Christ's headship within His mystical marriage to the Church. With these considerations in mind, let us turn to the sequential pattern of masculine desire.

Christ and the Masculine Pattern of Desire

Typological comparisons are not mere human constructions, concoctions, or strained connections, but rather are a mysterious kind of divine thread contained in the scriptures that artfully depict and testify to God's foreknowledge being actuated in human lives to fulfill His divine plan. Considering this, we will examine in broad strokes Christ's fulfillment of the aforementioned, patterned sequence—which was prefigured by Adam and St. Joseph—in our hope to unveil true masculine spiritual headship.

As mentioned previously, the pattern of *desire to fulfillment* begins with, first, a desire for something not yet given or acquired as demonstrated by Adam's desire for a suitable partner and St. Joseph's desire for the Virgin Mary; and second, a holy longing that is induced by man's desire not yet being fulfilled as with Adam not yet having Eve and St. Joseph seeking to separate himself from Mary after discovering her pregnant without his physical cooperation. Third, man experiences a personal solitude before God, wherein he realizes his helplessness and need for God to intervene as Adam depended upon God to fulfill his desire for a partner and as St. Joseph depended upon God to direct the course of his life regarding the Blessed Virgin Mary. Fourth, man undergoes a "rest" in God, wherein his faculties are not the force behind any resolution, but rather, by means of his rest, God is "permitted" to act. Indeed, it was not Adam that created Eve, but God who created her from him, and in a sense without him. St. Joseph was not to take a determined course of action regarding Mary, but rather God commanded him to act and take Mary as his wife. Fifth, man arises from his rest and receives the desired gift. As we will see, these five stages are exemplified dramatically in our Lord Jesus.

———

Besides the intense longing to fulfill His Father's will, within the Sacred Heart of Jesus burned a singular, great desire. Whereas Adam and St. Joseph longed for a bride that would complete them, our Lord Jesus desired to be the completion of His Bride, the

Church. Speaking of this ardent desire, Jesus said, "And I have a baptism wherewith I am to be baptized" (Lk 12:50).

> Jesus Christ reveals His abounding desire to give his life for love of us. He calls his death a baptism, because from it He will arise victorious never to die again.[139]

Indeed, our Lord burned not with selfish desire, but rather with the pure intention to sacrifice himself on behalf of humanity. The first stage of masculine desire is fulfilled perfectly by Christ, whose aspiration was, and is, most pure and disinterested. His intent was never to preserve His own life, but rather to lay down His life as a ransom for many.[140] This is the spirit of Christ: to love for the sake of the other, even at the cost of oneself. This is the indispensable foundation of male headship: to love one's wife and children as Christ loves us. If we have the spirit of the Lord Jesus, we too will burn with the desire to donate ourselves on behalf of the garden, the family. If we do not possess this gift, we must pray for it, for without it one is not far along the journey of masculine headship.

How can this be? Where there is a desire to sacrifice oneself

---

139 *Navarre Bible*, Commentary on Luke Chapter 12:50, 164.
140 See Mt 20:28; Mk 10:45.

for another, there exists the purest form of love, unhindered by selfishness. Where there is authentic self-giving love, there is true freedom. This freedom is the very strength of a man. The man who experiences this freedom for which Christ has set us free is no longer bound by self-preoccupation, or able to be bribed or bought off by worldly pursuits.[141] He is truly free to love, and by loving he is free truly.

As with Adam and St. Joseph, our Lord Jesus subjected himself to the process of bringing his desire to perfection in patience, not that our Lord was imperfect, or that his desire was impure, but rather our Lord demonstrated that waiting for an object of desire without grasping for it is an essential stage of masculine desire. Jesus perfected this process of working from *desire to fulfillment* to leave an example for us. Though "indeed he was the Son of God, he learned obedience by the things he suffered: And being consummated, he became, to all that obey him, the cause of eternal salvation" (Heb 5:8–9).

The word consummated is derived from the Greek root word *telos,* which conveys the concept of enduring many, necessary stages to reach an end goal.[142] This is also the word our Lord uses from the

---

141 See Gal 5:1.

142 *Telos,* meaning to bring to an end, to complete, perfect. "*Téleios* (an adjective, derived from *télos,* "consummated goal")—mature (consummated) from going through the necessary stages to reach the end-goal, i.e. developed into

Cross, indicating that His sacrifice for humanity was completed: "It is consummated" (Jn 19:30). In other words, if a man is to achieve completion and help to bring others—particularly his wife—to completion, he is to subject himself to the necessary stages that will aid him in reaching his ultimate goal, his ultimate sacrifice.

Additionally, the Greek word for patience, or to be patient, is *hupomoné*, which is comprised of two words: *hypó*, meaning under, and *ménō*, meaning to remain or endure. [143] The word *ménō*, or *menē*, is the word that our Lord uses on seven occasions in the fifteenth chapter of the Gospel of St. John, nearly pleading with his disciples to "remain" in Him.[144] It appears that the concept of remaining in Christ, under harsh circumstances, particularly that of a desire not yet fulfilled, is essential to seeing the spiritual journey to completion.

Indeed, my brother, you will be tempted to flee from the purifying process of becoming a true man of God. Yet, if you remain in Christ, God will use your desire for a woman to aid

---

a consummating completion by fulfilling the necessary process (spiritual journey); See *Telos*, Bible Hub, online edition, www.biblehub.com/greek/1760.htm, accessed 3/19/2020.

143 See *Hypomoné* , Bible Hub, online edition, www.biblehub.com/greek/5281.htm, accessed 3/19/2020. *Hypomoné* (from *hypó*, "under" and *ménō*, "remain, endure") —properly, remaining under, endurance; steadfastness, especially as God enables the believer to "remain (endure) under "the challenges He allots in life."

144 See Jn 15.

you in loving her authentically. Yet, this desire serves a greater purpose than simply loving the creature. By enduring the stages of *desire to fulfillment*, God infuses within the man the longing to sacrifice himself on behalf of God and for His family. Yet, a man must remain faithful, especially when the object of desire—whatever it is—is not being granted.

The second stage of Christ's desire not being yet fulfilled are indicated by His words "And how I am straitened until it is accomplished" (Lk 12:50). The Greek word for accomplished is *telesthē*, a form of *telos*, indicating, yet again, that our Lord has a singular goal: to bring to an end His earthly existence by completing his sacrifice. True accomplishment is completion that can only be obtained by donating oneself for the sake of another.

Our Lord's will is to complete and perfect, not only his mission, but also the object of his mission, His Bride, His Body of believers. It is during this second stage that God conditions man to cooperate in the process of sanctifying and purifying his motives for the purpose of gently leading him to become a man of sacrifice. If a man thwarts this process, or dismisses himself from it, his desires and motives will consistently be self-oriented. He will never be complete, *telos*, nor will his mission be accomplished, *telesthē*. When this occurs, a man will either cling to the woman for his identity or use her to quench his appetite for disordered gratifications. Thus, he will never reach completion, nor will he help complete his wife (and children), which is the goal of male headship.

If a man embraces this second stage, God will eventually lead him into the third stage of personal solitude, a dark night that appears to lack human and spiritual consolation. During our Lord's crucifixion, while experiencing the most horrific physical torment, He was literally hanging between Heaven and earth. This suspension also is a symbol of His spiritual torment. Our Lord could not be consoled by men of the earth (*adamah*), nor was He yet received by his Father in Heaven. He remained (*menē*) in the tension between Heaven and earth, enduring the darkest personal solitude. In his Gospel, St. Matthew recounts that "now from the sixth hour there was darkness over the whole earth, until the ninth hour" (Mt 27:45). This literal darkness that enveloped the earth during Christ's most bitter self-oblation is a symbol of the dark night wherein no consolation, either by man or by God, will be granted. Whereas Adam, in solitude, desired the creation of a bride, Christ in bitter solitude, during the ultimate season of darkness, yearned for the creation of His Bride, "which is his body, and the fullness of him who is filled all in all" (Eph 1:23).[145] This bitter dark night culminated with the Death of the Lord. As the psalmist prophetically described: "Lover and friend hast thou put far from me, and my only companion is darkness."[146]

After enduring this dark night, Christ entered the fourth stage of masculine desire: the deep sleep. As Adam underwent a supernatural slumber and St. Joseph entered a dream like state—both prior to God granting them their brides—our Lord Jesus, while hanging on the Cross, entered the deep sleep of death. At this moment, "one of the soldiers with a spear opened his side, and immediately there came out blood and water" (Jn 19:34).

St. Thomas notes that John

> Does not say wounded, but *opened*, because, in his side the door of eternal life is opened to us. . . . This event was also prefigured, for just as from the side of Christ, sleeping on the cross, there flowed blood and water, which makes the Church holy, *so from the side*

---

145 Notice that this passage describes the concept of the Body being the completion of Christ, by means of Christ completing the Body for He grants His Body His fullness. He is "all" in her, that all may be all-complete in Him.

146 Ps 88:18, *Roman Breviary*, Friday, Compline, Psalm 88:18.

of the sleeping Adam there was formed the woman, who prefigured the Church.[147]

And again, St. Augustine states:

Here the second Adam with bowed head slept upon the cross, that thence a wife might be formed from him, flowing from his side while He slept.[148]

Yet there is another connection between the sleep of Adam and the sleep of the final Adam:

Now there was in the place where [Jesus] was crucified, a garden; and in the garden a new sepulcher, wherein no man had ever been laid. There, therefore, because of the Jewish day of Preparation, as the tomb was close at hand, they laid Jesus there. (John 19:41–42)

As Adam was placed by God in the garden, where he entered a supernatural slumber during which the Lord formed the first

---

147 St. Thomas Aquinas, *Commentary on the Gospel of John*, 450 (emphasis added).
148 St. Augustine, *In Ioann, Evang.*, 120, 2.

woman from his side, similarly, while in a garden, our Lord's side was opened as He underwent the sleep of death, resting on the Sabbath. Even in His death, our Lord fulfills the Law.

Adam, after waking from his sleep, received Eve, and St. Joseph, after waking from his dream, received Mary; in a similar way Jesus, in the garden, rose from the dead and eventually encountered the first representative of the Bride, Mary Magdalene. This constitutes the fifth stage of desire: waking to receive the object of desire. Yet, we must be clear: Christ did not desire the Bride for Himself, but rather desired that He be given to His Bride.

It was Mary who "came to the tomb early, while it was still dark, and saw that the stone had been taken away from the tomb" (Jn 20:1). Realizing that the body of Jesus was missing, Mary returned to Sts. Peter and John, explaining what she had witnessed. Peter and John ran to the tomb, and, after finding the tomb as Mary had described it, they "Departed again to their homes" (Jn 20:10).

At this point, Mary Magdalene remained outside the tomb weeping, when suddenly our Lord appeared to her. Mary Magdalene truly represents the Bride in both her sinfulness—having seven demons—and her redeemed spiritual beauty. Indeed, we can associate the words of the bride in the Canticle of Canticles with Mary Magdalene, and all those who constitute the Body of Christ: "I am black but beautiful" (Sg 1:4). And again:

In my bed by night I sought him whom my soul loveth: I sought him, and found him not. I will rise, and will go about the city: in the streets and the broad ways I will seek him whom my soul loveth: I sought him, and I found him not. The watchmen who keep the city found me: Have you seen him, whom my soul loveth? When I had a little passed by them, I found him whom my soul loveth: I held him: and I will not let him go. (Song of Songs 3:1–4)

The bride in the canticle is a figure of Mary Magdalene, who seeks her bridegroom, the one she loves, in the darkness of night, prior to dawn. She had scarcely passed the watchmen of the infant Church, Sts. Peter and John, when she found Him whom her soul loved. As the bride in the canticle clings to her groom, so also Mary Magdalene clings to Christ.

Prefigured by the first man (Adam) and the just man (St. Joseph), Jesus, the God-man, fulfills the stages of masculine desire, bringing them to completion. By ascending to His Father, He obtained for us the Holy Spirit that redeems, sanctifies, and animates us, enabling us to fulfill these stages of masculine desire.

Our Lord completed His mission, obtaining the Spirit for His

Bride, who makes her one with her Head, that is Christ. Thus, the Lord completes his mission by completing His bride.

Headship: At the Service of Completing the Bride

At the heart of a husband's vocational mission is the responsibility of tending to his wife's completion in Christ. The husband's efforts to help complete his wife have a reciprocal benefit: As he strives to complete his wife, his wife will help to complete him. God has ordained that the two, the husband and wife, "shall be two in one flesh. This is a great sacrament; but I speak in Christ and in the church." (Eph 5:32). The ultimate reason for any married couple's human existence is to become a sign that participates in, and directs humanity to, the mystical marriage of Christ and His Church. The more perfected the unity of husband and wife, the more effective is the couple's transmission of Christ's love for His Church to others and to themselves. This is important. God does not use the couple as a symbol to direct the world to Himself without blessing the couple with the fruits of communion with Him. The fruits of a marriage in Christ and the sacramental symbol of marriage pointing to Christ are interrelated, and as one increases so also does the other.

The progress of this unity is dependent upon the husband and wife responding to divine grace and participating together toward Christian unity. However, upon the man is the burden of sacrificial responsibility. Indeed, the husband is to continually strive to set the pace of self-giving love in his marriage. This sacrificial responsibility that tends toward full unity in Christ can also be referred to as male headship.

However, male headship has been so closely associated with patriarchal domination, misogyny, and female objectification that the term is believed to be an anti-Christian concept, or a means by which one can invalidate Christianity.

Yet, Christ is Head of the Church, and the scriptures attest to the fact that man, in the image of Christ, is head of his wife. To identify headship with tyranny is to identify the Lord Jesus as a tyrant. In other words, we cannot deny headship without denying Christ. Therefore, if we are to embrace the true Christ, we must embrace the true headship of a husband.

If we are to understand male headship accurately, it is imperative that we familiarize ourselves with, and perhaps penetrate—even minimally—the mystery of Christ's mystical marriage to his Church. The holy Apostle proclaims that the husband's headship is analogous to Christ's headship of the Church.[149]

---

149 See Eph 5:23.

This raises the questions: What is the headship of a husband, and of what does it consist?

By knowing and embracing those characteristics embodied in Christ's headship, we may have a real participation in his headship, which is at the service of the completion of marriage and the family. In other words, a husband's headship is at the service of bringing his wife and children to completion. This demands that the man allow the circumstances of his marriage and fatherhood to forge him into a complete man of God.

The Greek word for head used by St. Paul in several of his letters is *kephale*, which literally means head and can be interpreted as director or chief. However, the way this word is continually used by the holy Apostle in reference to Christ is interpreted as source or beginning or *completion*, or one who *brings fullness*. There are two key passages that speak of the husband as *kephale*, head of the wife: 1 Corinthians 11:3 and Ephesians 5:23. Here the word *kephale* carries the same meaning, in an analogous sense, that it has in those passages in which it is applied to Christ.[150] In other

---

150 "Let's start with the scriptural command that the husband is to be 'head' of his wife. The Greek word used by the sacred writer is *kephale*, which literally means 'head.' When we use the word head figuratively, we mean 'leader' or 'chief' or 'director'; the one who has authority in a given situation or structure. In other words, the head is the boss. There are seven passages in Paul's epistles in which *kephale* is used figuratively. Five of them refer to Christ as 'head' of the Church (Eph 1:22–23; 4:15; Col 1:18; 2:9–10, 19). Here *kephale* used figuratively means 'exalted originator and completer,' 'source or beginning or completion,'

words, a husband's headship is analogous to Christ's headship, not as a boss or a chief, but as one who strives to bring to his wife and family to completion in Christ.

Here, again, we find the re-occurring theme of completion closely associated with a husband's meaning and mission. A husband cares for his garden, cultivating it toward completion

---

or 'one who brings fullness.' There are other Greek words that mean 'boss' in our sense of the term. None is used to describe Christ's relationship to the Church—only *kephale* is. Two passages speak of the husband as kephale, 'head,' of the wife: 1 Corinthians 11:3 and Ephesians 5:23. Here the word kephale carries the same meaning, in an analogous sense that it has in those passages in which it is applied to Christ. Paul often used the head-body metaphor to stress the unity of Christ and his Church. In nature, of course, head and body are dependent on each other for their fullness. See in Ephesians 5:25–27 what Christ as kephale of the Church does for her: 'Christ loved the church and *gave himself up for her*, that he might sanctify her. . . that he might present the church to himself in splendor . . . that she might be holy and without blemish.' Christ gave himself up for the church to enable her to become all that God created her to be. Now look at what the husband's being kephale for his wife means: 'Husbands, love your wives, as Christ loved the church and gave himself up for her' (emphasis added). Not many husbands are called upon to literally die for their wives, but all husbands are called by God to sacrificially serve their wives. It is clear from Scripture that the husband's being head of his wife does not mean he is to be 'boss' or that he is to dominate his wife. Being 'head' means giving his wife sensitive, intelligent leadership. But note: It's to a leadership that grows out of loving consultation between the spouses. As head, the husband provides for and cares for his wife (and of course the children). *He bears primary overall responsibility for the family.* According to Scripture, there is only one way in which a husband can truly serve his wife as head: 'The head of every man is Christ, the head of a woman is her husband, and the head of Christ is God." In order to be truly head of his family, a husband must himself be submitted to Jesus Christ. His service as head consists above all in his responsibility to mediate the love of Jesus Christ to his wife and children.'" Catholic Answers, "Wives Be Subject to Your Husbands," https://www.catholic.com/magazine/print-edition/wives-be-subject-to-your-husbands, accessed 3/19/2020.

in Christ, which is evident by the fruit that the garden bears. "By their fruits you shall know them." (Mt 7:16). Your domestic garden is called to "bring forth fruit; and your fruit should remain." (Jn 15:16).

Jesus the Bridegroom

Headship is synonymous with the bridegroom or the husband. Christ is Head of His Body, the Church, and he is her Bridegroom.

> The theme of Christ as Bridegroom of the Church was prepared by the prophets and announced by John the Baptist (Jn 3:29). The Lord referred to himself as the "bridegroom" (Mk 2:19). The Apostle speaks of the whole Church and of each of the faithful members of his Body, as bride "betrothed" to Christ the Lord so as to become but one spirit with him (cf. Mt 22:1–14; 25:1–13; 1 Cor 6:15–17; 2 Cor 11:2). The Church is the spotless bride of the spotless Lamb (cf Rev 22:17; Eph 1:4, 5:27). "Christ loved the Church and gave himself up for her that he might sanctify her" (Eph 5:25–26). He has joined her with himself in an everlasting covenant and never stops caring for her as for his own body (cr. Eph 5:29). (*CCC*, 796)

The mystery of Christ's fidelity to His Bride, the Church, and this mystical union can be understood analogously through the lens of human marriage. Marriage, even with its failings, offers us a context by which we can understand Christ's faithfulness to His bride, the Church. Marriage between a man and a woman is inseparably linked to Christ's marriage to His Church.[151] Yet, the mystery of Christ and His Church must be meditated upon and applied to human marriage with great care lest we reduce this mystical marriage to mere human characteristics or exalt human marriage beyond its natural, or even its sublimated, supernatural capacity.

By its very nature, the nuptial analogy maintains a similarity, while also maintaining a greater dissimilarity, and, therefore, it is limited.[152] Yet, despite its limitation, it is perhaps the least limited analogy by which man can peer into the sacred communion between God and man. Therefore, if we are to comprehend the value

---

151 "The Church cannot therefore be understood as the mystical body of Christ, as the sign of man's covenant with God in Christ, or as the universal sacrament of salvation, unless we keep in mind the 'great mystery' involved in the creation of man as male and female and the vocation of both to conjugal love, to fatherhood and motherhood. The 'great mystery,' which is the Church and humanity in Christ, does not exist apart from the 'great mystery' expressed in the 'one flesh' . . . reality of marriage and the family." *Letter to Families*, 19.

152 "The mystery remains transcendent in regard to this analogy as in regard to any other analogy whereby we seek to express it in human language. At the same time, however, this analogy offers the possibility of a certain . . . 'penetration' into the very essence of the mystery." John Paul II, General Audience Nov 30, 1980).

and importance of our role and responsibility as men, it is imperative that we understand and appreciate the significance and beauty of marriage as instituted and redeemed by Christ. For if a man does not appreciate marriage, he cannot value his own headship. Marriage is not at the service of headship, but headship is at the service of marriage; and marriage is at the service of Christ.

Christ's Reclaiming Marriage

According to St. John's Gospel, Christ's public ministry began with His first public miracle at a wedding. This fact alone would be enough evidence to maintain the belief that Christ not only supports marriage but endorses it as having supreme significance in the Savior's plan for the redemption of mankind. To validate this proposition thoroughly, let us examine in detail St. John's account of our Lord's first public miracle and the context in which it occurred. By doing so, we will attempt to unveil the rich symbolism and meaning contained in this most inspired passage.

The following meditation will not only confirm the goodness and vitality of marriage, but, perhaps more fundamentally, demonstrate why it is imperative that we men reverence this sacrament and assume responsibility for this divinely instituted gift.

The opening line of St. John's Gospel begins, "In the beginning was the Word" (Jn 1:1). The phrase "in the beginning" echoes the first divinely inspired sentence in Sacred Scripture contained in the Book of Genesis: "In the beginning" (Gn 1:1). As with the Gospel writers Sts. Matthew and Luke, it appears that St. John is making an obvious connection between the creation accounts described in Genesis and the beginning of his Gospel.

St. John's Gospel gradually reveals a "new genesis" that, like the original creation account, spans seven days: The first day is described in verses 1–28. The second day begins in verse 29 with the phrase "the next day," and then proceeds with the description of this second day up to verse 34. The third day begins in verse 35 with the words "the next day." And the fourth day begins in verse 43 with the words "the following day." At this point, St. John's Gospel has recounted the transpiration of four days since "the beginning."

The second chapter, which recounts Christ's first public miracle at the Wedding at Cana, begins with the words "and the third day, there was a marriage in Cana of Galilee: and the mother of Jesus was there" (Jn 2:1). This third day, when added to the preceding four days, indicates that the event of the marriage at Cana of Galilee occurred on the seventh day. This seventh day was pre-figured by the seventh day of the original Genesis creation account when God made a covenant with man by means of the seventh day rest.

The Hebrew word for seven, *sheva,* can be interpreted to mean to swear an oath, to fill, to complete. In other words, on the seventh day, the first man and woman enter a covenant with God (a type of oath between persons), wherein God gives Himself to man that man may in turn give himself to God. Not only are the seven days of creation completed, but also God completes creation by making a covenant with man. In a sense, this is a mystical marriage between God and the first husband and wife. There is a profound connection between the Sacrament of Matrimony and the completion of the man and woman.

The Wedding at Cana, which occurred on the seventh day, is a symbolic fulfillment of God's "marriage" to mankind, established by means of his covenant with man on the seventh day of creation. This Wedding Feast at Cana appears to be a rich symbol of the original covenant between God and man, wherein the wine, which can be interpreted as a symbol of grace, runs dry. Indeed, the covenant between God and the original couple—soon after it was established—was ruptured by the Fall. The grace of God, His likeness in man, was lost—it had run out. In a sense, that which was complete (the original covenant) became incomplete by man's disobedience to God and therefore was in need of completion.

St. John indicates that both Jesus and His Mother attended this marriage. It is the Mother of Jesus who said to Him, "They have no wine" (Jn 2:3), meaning that just as the couple had run out of wine amidst the marriage feast, so also, figuratively, mankind ran out of sanctifying grace and is in need of new wine, which is redemptive grace.

"And Jesus saith to her 'Woman, what is that to me and to thee? my hour has not come'" (Jn 2:4). The fact that Jesus referred to his Mother as "Woman" at the moment she indicated that the wine, a symbol of grace, had run out is highly significant.

Recall that shortly after the moment when Adam and Eve squandered the grace of God, breaking God's covenant by means of an act of mistrust of the Father, God prophetically said to the serpent:

> I will put enmities between thee and the woman, and thy seed and her seed: she shall crush thy head, and thou shalt lie in wait for her heel. (Genesis 3:15)

The woman has consistently and traditionally been understood as

> The Blessed Virgin Mary, the New Eve, the mother of the Redeemer, who shares by anticipation and preeminently in the victory over her Son. Sin never

left its mark on her and the Church proclaims her as the Immaculate Conception.[153]

Eve did not crush the head of the serpent, the devil,[154] rather, she succumbed to the devil's seductions, whereas the New Eve, Mary, did not.

From these considerations, it seems more than plausible that the "marriage" between God and mankind, as established with, and represented by, Adam and Eve, was in need of new wine— grace. Therefore, the New Eve and the New and Final Adam were present at this new wedding as representatives of the human race for the purpose of re-establishing a final marriage covenant between Christ and His Church.

St. John mentions that there were set "six waterpots of stone. . . . Jesus saith to [the waiters]: Fill the waterpots with water" (Jn 2:6–7).

These six stone jars appear to be a rich symbol of the six days of creation. Yet, there is a marked distinction between the first six days of creation and this symbol. During the first creation account, God created man without man, yet the six water jars

153 *Navarre Bible*, Commentary on Genesis Chapter 3:16, p 55.
154 The Book of Revelation connects the ancient serpent of the Genesis account with the devil. The two are one and the same. "And he laid hold on the dragon the old serpent, which is the devil and Satan, and bound him for a thousand years" (Rev 20:2).

and the servant's participation in filling them express symbolically that our Lord will not re-create, redeem, or re-establish God's mystical marriage with man without man's cooperation.

This seems to be indicated by Jesus' command to the waiters to "fill the waterpots with water" (Jn 2:6) and also the servers' response to his divine command: "They filled them up to the brim" (Jn 2:7).

The phrase "fill them to the brim" appears to indicate that the divine Savior desires our full participation in the re-establishing of the New Covenant.

This ordinary water is a symbol of man's nature and natural capacity. Despite the excellence of man's works, his efforts—without grace—remain common, ordinary water. Grace is necessary to perfect nature and man's works. Without grace a man cannot win his salvation or redemption.[155]

Christ's transformation of the water into wine depicts the marriage between grace and nature, faith and works, and God and man. Again, according to St. Augustine, "The God, who created you without you, will not save you without you." Man cannot by his own good works procure his salvation or perfec-

---

[155] "Since therefore grace does not destroy nature but perfects it, natural reason should minister to faith as the natural bent of the will ministers to charity." St. Thomas Aquinas, *Summa Theologica*, I, Q. 1, Art. 8, Resp. to Obj. 2.

tion, but God will not perfect him or save him without his good works. St. Augustine's words remind us, "God crowns his own merits in us."[156]

This new marriage contracted by God between Christ and His Church far supersedes the original covenant that God made with our original parents. This is indicated by the chief steward's words to the bridegroom (who is a symbol of Christ, the Bridegroom) after realizing that Jesus has changed the water into wine:

> Every man at first setteth forth good wine, and when men have well drunk, then that which is worse. But thou hast kept the good wine until now. (John 2:10)

The new wine that the Bridegroom provides, which far surpasses the first batch of wine served, is a symbol of the superseding, redemptive grace obtained by our Lord Jesus' sacrifice at Calvary. This New Covenant far exceeds the Old Covenant. As St. John poetically expresses earlier in his Gospel, "And of his fullness we all have received, grace [upon] grace. For the Law was given by Moses; grace and truth came by Jesus Christ" (Jn 1:16–17).

---

156 St. Augustine. Marcus Dodds, 1876-Theology.

The account of the Wedding at Cana ends with John stating that "this beginning of miracles did Jesus in Cana of Galilee; and manifested his glory, and his disciples believed in him" (Jn 2:11).

The word manifested in Greek is *ephanerōsen,* is related to the word *epiphany,* meaning an appearance or manifestation of a divine being and also an intuitive grasp of reality through something (such as an event) usually simple and striking.[157] Indeed, Christ uses the usual event of a wedding to manifest his divine being and also His ardent desire to establish a new covenant, a new "marriage" with mankind.

From these considerations, we also discern the tenderness of God who doesn't blot out that which is broken and begin fresh *ex nihilo.* Our Lord does not erase the covenant established with Adam and Eve, which was eventually re-affirmed and ratified with Moses, but rather fulfills it, redeems it, and transforms it. The transformation of the water into wine is a figure of Christ's ability to transform the Old Covenant into the New and everlasting Covenant.

My brother, how important it is that we understand this point. Christ does not destroy that which has failed or is broken, but rather redeems it and sanctifies it. "Great shall be the glory of this last house more than of the first, saith the Lord of hosts:

---

157 Manifested. In Merriam-Webster's online dictionary. Retrieved from http://www.merriam-webster.com/dictionary/epiphany, accessed 3/19/2020.

and in this place I will give peace, saith the Lord of hosts" (Hg 2:10). Though your life may consist of considerable failings, sufferings, and setbacks, you must never doubt the mercy of God who can and will use the "fallen temple" of your life to build a greater temple in which His glory dwells. The Lord does not desire to destroy what pre-exists in man—but to redeem and transform it for His glory.

Israel Transformed into The New Israel: The Church

The concept and reality of our Lord's desire not to destroy that which exists, but rather to use that which exists, even if broken, to redeem and transform it for His glory is beautifully articulated in figurative language by St. Luke's historical recounting of two of our Lord's miracles weaved into one single account.

Jarius, a ruler of a synagogue, begged Jesus to come to his house:

> For he had an only daughter, almost twelve years old, and she was dying. And it happened as [Jesus] went that he was thronged by the multitudes. And there was a certain woman having an issue of blood [for] twelve years, who had bestowed all her substance

on physicians, and could not be healed by any. (Luke 8:42–43)

The two accounts of the hemorrhaging woman and the synagogue official's daughter are integrated into one episode that contains a common theme of "twelve years." It appears that St. Luke, by integrating these two miracles of two females— one being an older woman who has hemorrhaged for twelve years, and the other being a daughter who died at the age of twelve years—is, with one master stroke, communicating a compelling truth.

The hemorrhaging woman is a figure of Israel, comprised of twelve tribes, who was spiritually hemorrhaging from within. Indeed, when the Romans, under the command of Titus, besieged Rome in AD 70, the invading soldiers discovered that the inhabitants of Jerusalem were submerged in strife and inner conflict, divided and devouring their own.[158]

The synagogue official's twelve-year-old daughter is a figure of the Church of Christ, founded on the Twelve Apostles, which is raised by our Lord from the nearly dead, broken, and hemorrhaging Israel. By means of these symbols, one can deduce that our Lord's desire was not to destroy the Twelve

---

158 Flavius Josephus, The Antiquities of the Jews, Translated by William Whiston.

Tribes of Israel, but rather to redeem and transform them into the New Israel, the Church, the Bride of Christ. Indeed, St. John, in the Book of Revelation describes a vision of the Bride of Christ:

> The holy city Jerusalem coming down out of heaven from God, having the glory of God . . . and it has a wall great and high having twelve gates, and in the gates twelve angels, and names written thereon, which are the names of the twelve tribes of the children of Israel. And the wall of the city had twelve foundations, and in them, the twelve names of the twelve apostles of the Lamb. (Revelation 21:10–14)

It is obvious from this vision that God did not erase the people of God, Israel, who preceded the Church, but rather redeemed them and transformed them into the New Israel, the Church.

These considerations grant us the ability to catch a glimpse of the value and significance our Lord imparts to marriage. By his miraculous transformation of water into wine at the marriage of Cana, our Lord demonstrated his desire to heal and redeem and *sacramentalize* marriage. From the moment of Christ's first public miracle, the human institution of marriage is blessed by

Christ as a sacrament, a human symbol that is a channel for divine grace.

In addition to this, the number twelve has often been interpreted as meaning completeness. Jesus desires to complete his Bride, the Church. Yet, Luke intentionally mentions that Jairus's daughter, a symbol of the Church rising from the hemorrhaging Israel, is approximately twelve years old. The word *approximately* can indicate that the filling of the stone jars has yet to be completed by Christ's Church. The servants, the Church, must labor to fill them to the brim. It does not indicate that Christ's redemptive work is lacking, but rather that our participation in that work is needed. Here again, it must be noted, that the completion of the bride is closely associated with the role and responsibility of headship as verified by Christ.

My brother, from these miraculous events, we learn that if we are to be like the Bridegroom, it is imperative that we participate in Christ's will to redeem, heal, and transform our marriages that they become a sacramental sign, a witness to this world of the ultimate marriage of Christ and His Church.

Completion of the Body, the Bride

God united himself to humanity in order that humanity could be united to God. The Word became permanently fixed to flesh for all eternity to ensure that all flesh may be united to the Word eternally. This integration of God and man, the divine and human natures, in the Person of Jesus Christ (defined as the hypostatic union), will never cease to exist. If Christ would suddenly separate his divine nature from his human nature, our human nature would cease to be linked to God's divine nature. Christ, forever, presents his perfected, sacrificial, human nature in union with His divine nature to God the Father.[159] God the Father looks upon Christ's perfected humanity and sees all of humanity perfected and acceptable in Him. Without Christ's eternal divine nature hypostatically united to His human nature, human nature cannot be linked or acceptable to God.

The mission of the eternal Bridegroom is to complete His Bride with His Spirit that she may become a "partaker in the divine nature."[160]

> The Apostle speaks of the whole Church and each
> of the faithful members of His Body, as a bride "be-
> trothed" to Christ the Lord so as to become one spirit

---

159 "Whereby he is able also to save for ever them that come to God by him; always living to make intercession for us." Heb 7:25.

160 See 2 Pt 1:4.

with him (cf. Mt 22:1–14; 25:1–13; 1 Cor 6:15–17; 2 Cor 11:2). (*CCC*, 796)

Christ and His Church together comprise the "whole Christ" (*Christus totus*). (*CCC*, 795)

Yet, in this *Christus totus* is a personal distinction:

The unity of Christ and the Church, head and members of one Body, also implies the distinction of the two within a personal relationship. (*CCC*, 796)

In this relationship Christ is Head and the Church are the members of the Body. As St. Augustine said:

Do you understand and grasp, brethren, God's grace toward us? Marvel and rejoice we have become Christ. For if He the head, we are the members; He and we together are the whole man . . . The fullness of Christ then is the head and the members. But what does "head and members mean? Christ and the Church (St. Augustine, *In Jo. ev.* 21, 8 PL 35, 1568). (*CCC*, 795)

God has indeed "subjected all things under his feet, and hath made him *head* over all the church, which is his body, and fullness of him who is filled all in all" (Eph 1:22–23, emphasis added).

The marital analogy, threaded through the New Testament, indicates that the heart of Christ's mission is to complete His Bride, His Church, in Himself, that she may be full of Him and become one with Him.

Yet, the analogy poses a spiritual challenge to men, for the mystery of Christ and His Church is figured analogously by a marriage between a man and a woman. God, in His relationship with his Church, is always the initiator, and the human person is the receiver of His love and attention.[161] In this way, a man is analogously like the "bride" of Christ; he is "bride" in relationship to Christ.

However, the man receives from Christ his responsibility and office as head of his wife "because the husband is the head of the wife, as Christ is head of the church" (Eph 5:23). A man, by means of his own marriage to his wife, symbolizes Christ as head, while also being "bride" in relationship to the Bridegroom, Jesus Christ. He must be both. If a man is not the bride of Christ, he cannot truly be Christ to his bride. If a man is not

---

161 "In this is charity: not as though we had loved God, but because he hath first loved us, and sent his Son to be a propitiation for our sins." 1 Jn 4:10.

the Body of Christ, who is the head, the man cannot be head, or Christ, to "his body," his wife.

By being the bride of Christ, a man learns how to be dependent on Christ his Head and therefore gains insight into how he ought to love his wife, who depends on him. As justice is tempered by mercy, so a man's strength is tempered by tenderness, which He learns by allowing himself to be loved tenderly by Christ.

Some men conditioned by a machismo attitude cannot accept this teaching. Yet, by rejecting Christ's tenderness, a man can become susceptible to becoming a tyrant, distant, insensitive, or lacking a compassionate disposition in his headship for he forgets to love his wife as God loves him.

Regardless, the husband is head of his wife. If, for whatever reason, whether it be from fear of failure, concern that headship somehow subordinates his wife, or misunderstanding that such a role is counter-cultural—he neglects this responsibility and, thus, neglects his divine calling.

A Case for Headship

Archbishop Fulton Sheen said that "there are not one hundred people in the United States who hate the Catholic Church, but there are millions who hate what they wrongly perceive the

Catholic Church to be."[162] In a similar manner, there are millions who condemn male headship for what they wrongly perceive it to be, and very few people that hate male headship for what it is truly.

Considering this, it is imperative to define male headship, what it is, and its roots and origin, while also referring to the scriptural and magisterial support of this divinely instituted vocation.

Before proceeding, it is vital that we declare what male headship is not. Male headship is not masculine tyranny or domination of the woman. A husband's headship does not indicate any type of inequality in nature or being among the sexes; it is not misogynistic, nor subordinationism; and it certainly does not dismiss the man from being responsible to God and accountable to his wife.

Unfortunately, there exist many Church leaders who avoid referring to the scriptural passages that clearly communicate the mandate for male headship as being intrinsic to marital and familial order. Still others utilize the short form provided in the Lectionary, and thus avoid reading those particular passages from the pulpit for the purpose of not offending women. Still others attempt to interpret those passages in a way that neglects

---

162 Archbishop Fulton J. Sheen, Preface for *Radio Replies* (1938).

to say anything definitive about male headship other than the husband and the wife have equal dignity and authority.

In their efforts to defend and propagate woman's rights, they maintain that the sexes were created simultaneously, as the first creation account indicates, while dismissing the second creation account altogether, which demonstrates that the woman was created by God after the man, and from the man.

For the purpose of intentionally aiding men in their role as husbands and fathers, it is essential that a full vision of the headship of a husband is articulated. Rather than reiterating the reality of equal dignity of men and women (which is proclaimed by the Church) and that women are fully capable of fulfilling professional roles that men have traditionally occupied, we will be specifically focusing on what male headship is, rather than what it is not. This is very important. Men, over the last century, have been told what male headship isn't, rather than what it actually is. Because of this absence of teaching, men have attempted to re-define themselves and their masculinity in light of the culture and its ever-changing trends.

It is imperative that we discover the essence of man, the husband and father, by investigating the creation accounts accurately, rather than apologizing for the man being created as God intended him to be. Therefore, we will investigate both creation accounts with the hope of gaining greater clarity regarding man; whether God created him to be different than woman; and whether he has a unique role that is distinct from the woman.

The Beginning and Origin of the Man

In the first creation account, God is quoted as saying, "Let us make man to our image and likeness . . . and God created man to his own image: to the image of God he created him: male and female he created them" (Gn 1:26–27). This scripture can, on the surface, appear to demonstrate that God created the man and woman simultaneously. Though this is a plausible interpretation, a couple of details contained in this succinct text ought to be highlighted.

The sacred author lists the creation of man in three segments: first, the writer says that God created man, in Hebrew *ha'adam* ("and God created man [*ha'adam*] to his own image" [Gn 1:27]). *Ha'adam* is not a personal pronoun or name, but rather a generic or universal term indicating humanity in an impersonal sense. The second segment of the passage proceeds to say, "To the image of God he created him ('ō·tōw)" (Gn 1:27), indicating male sexuality; and then God finalizes the thought with the third segment: "Male and female he created them ('ō·tām)" (Gn 1:27), indicating a distinction between the sexes.

It appears that the author of the first creation account is conveying that humanity in a general sense, as defined by the impersonal pronoun *ha'adam*, was created in the image of God. Then the man as signified by "him" is listed first, and prior to the woman, as created in the image and likeness of God; and afterward the woman is added to constitute "them."

Later in Genesis, the author says that "Pharaoh sent him ('ō·tōw) [Abraham], with his wife ('iš·tōw)" (Gn 12:20), which appears to indicate that the person who is identified in the first creation account as 'ō·tōw is male. In addition to this, the sacred writer says that Adam "called the name of his wife ('iš·tōw) Eve" (Gn 3:20).

In other words, one may conclude from the first creation account that God created the man and woman simultaneously. However, it appears that a creative order is established, affording also the interpretation that the man was created prior to the woman.

Again, as with the first creation account, the second creation account has been interpreted as man, a non-personal human being, created first, and then, afterward, the sexes were created simultaneously. Prior to the creation of woman, the man is referred to as *ha'adam*, an impersonal, gender neutral, representation of humanity. It is only after the deep sleep of *ha'adam*, and God removing the rib from the side of *ha'adam*, that the man is referred to as *ish* (man, husband) and the woman as *ish shah* (woman, wife). Some contend that the text indicates that God imparted humanity with sexuality only after the sleep of *ha'adam*.

However, one problem with interpreting the account this way is that after the creation of the woman, the man is still referred to as *ha'adam* repeatedly. In fact, it is *ha'adam* (Adam) himself, who is quoted as saying that *ish shah* (woman, wife) was taken from *ish*. This indicates that Adam understood that his sexuality existed before and after the creation of Eve for he referred to himself as both *ha'adam* and *ish* ("And Adam [*ha'adam*] said: This now is bone of my bones, and flesh of my flesh; she shall be called woman [*ish shah*], because she was taken out of man [*ish*]" [Gn 2:23]).

In addition to this, Adam continues to be identified by the sacred writer as *ha'adam* in latter passages such as "he (*ha'adam*) shall have dominion over thee" (Gn 3:16). In this case, it is God using the original name *ha'adam*, which is translated in this verse as husband. In other words, God and Adam both refer to the husband and man, Adam, as *ha'adam*, indicating that male sexuality was given to the man prior to the sleep of Adam and the creation of woman.

When only a pine tree exists, a person simply identifies it as that "tree" in an impersonal non-distinct way. In such a context, there is no need to make a descriptive distinction to distinguish the tree from other types of its own species. Yet, when that pine tree is situated among oak trees, a distinction is demanded to indicate which tree is being referred to; a descriptive word must be added.

In a similar way, prior to the creation of Eve, man was identified indistinctly for there was no reason to refer to him as different in his gender (no other distinction was demanded because the female had not been created, but only in his distinction from the animals); therefore he was called *ha'adam.* After the creation of woman, however, a distinction had to be made, lest the two beings be interpreted as the same sex. This appears to be a valid interpretation of the second creation account.

Though one may hold to the idea that *ha'adam* was an impersonal, perhaps gender-neutral being (though Adam being gender-neutral would be contrary to Catholic theology due to the idea that sex is an aspect of the soul, which was given to Adam at the moment of his creation outside the garden) prior to Adam's *tardemah* (deep sleep), it is not supported by Scripture.

For example, St. Paul who was fluent in Hebrew and had a significant understanding of the Old Testament, said, "[Man] is the image and glory of God; but the woman is the glory of the man. For man is not of the woman, but the woman is of the man" (1 Cor 11:7–11). Again, "Adam was first formed; then Eve" (1 Tm 2:13).

The Pauline understanding of the creation account is also reflected in the early Church's Apostolic Constitutions:

> The "man is head of the woman" (1 Cor 11:3), and he is originally ordained for the priesthood; it is not just to abrogate the order of the creation and leave the first to come to the last part of the body. For the woman is the body of the man, taken from his side and subject to him, from whom she was separated for procreation of children. For he says, "He shall rule over you (Gen 3:16). For the first part of the woman is the man, as being her head."[163]

The differences between the first and second creation accounts can be likened to a macro-view as compared to a micro-view of creation. The first account is viewed in brief, with broad strokes, almost from afar, while the second account is a detailed analysis that penetrates the psychological dimensions and inner subjectivity of man and woman both prior to, and after, the Fall.

This comparison can be likened to two recollections of a

---

163 *Apostolic Constitutions* 3:1–9 (c. AD 400).

wedding. The first recounts that the couple stood at the same time before the altar while exchanging their vows. The second account reveals in full detail that the groom awaited his bride, standing alone in front of the altar. Then, after a moment of silence, his bride entered the church and proceeded to walk up the aisle toward him. Then after they met before the altar, they exchanged their wedding vows.

Both accounts describe the fact that the couple was married, and there exists no contradiction between the two. Yet, if one was to hold to the idea that the woman and man arrived at the altar simultaneously, the person would be in error, neglecting to accept the series of events as they actually transpired, according to the more detailed second account.

It appears that the modern emphasis on translating the second creation account to indicate that God gave Adam male genitalia and a masculine soul at the moment that He formed Eve is an intentional effort to support the equality of the sexes, while avoiding the reality of male headship and the responsibility associated with it.

One need not deny male headship for the purpose of upholding equal dignity between husband and wife. To believe that headship endows a greater dignity to the man would be to believe erroneously in something that closely resembles subordinationism.

Subordinationism is "a group of heresies that hold that the Son and the Holy Spirit are subordinate to the Father in nature and being. . . . not to be confused with the view that the Son and Spirit are subordinate to the Father in their procession (the Son eternally proceeds from the Father and the Spirit from the Father and Son) and in their missions (both to do the will of the Father). It is their nature and being that are in question."[164]

In a similar way, the Son and the Spirit are not less than the Father in nature and being, but equal in essence. Both the Son and the Holy Spirit, however, are subordinate in procession. Analogously, woman is equal in nature and being to the man; though she came forth from the man. Additionally, a child's dignity is equal to his or her parents, yet the child is subordinate in terms of procession from its parents.

To deny the idea that the woman was created after and from the man, one would need to interpret St. Paul, the Church's teaching, and the authors of Sacred Scripture as meaning something that they did not intend to say.

---

164 *The Fathers Know Best*, Jimmy Akin (San Diego, CA: Catholic Answers, 2010).

Additionally, the entire body of Scripture appears to be consistent on this point:

A woman, if she have superiority, is contrary to her husband. (Eccl 25:30)

But I would have you know, that the head of every man is Christ; and the head of the woman is the man; and the head of Christ is God. (1 Cor 11:3)

But I suffer not a woman . . . to use authority over the man. . . . For Adam was first formed; then Eve. (1 Tm 2:12–13)

[Women] to be . . . obedient to their husbands, that the word of God be not blasphemed. (Ti 2:5)

In a like manner also let wives be subject to their husbands: that if any believe not the word, they may be won without the word, by the conversation of the wives. (1 Pt 3:1)

Wives, be subject to your husbands, as it behoveth in the Lord. (Col 3:18)

Let women be subject to their husbands, as to the Lord: Because the husband is head of the wife, as Christ is head of the Church. (Eph 5:22–23)

Rather than attempting to dismiss the biblical, traditional, and divinely ordained reality of a husband's headship, we ought to discern how to understand, teach, and live this sacred summons according to God's plan.

Mutual Submission and Authentic Male Headship

If male headship is to be true in character, it must reflect and participate in Christ's headship. The divine Word lowered himself to the human level for the purpose of raising humanity, as His Body, to the divine level. He accomplishes the elevation of His Bride to the divine level by loving the Church with relentless, self-giving, unconditional love.

A husband, though not superior to his wife in nature and being, nevertheless has been granted a unique and conditional primacy in his authority, which is at the service of elevating and upholding her beauty, dignity, and person. The husband must follow the example of Christ, who lowered himself. Yet, whereas Christ's condescension involved an emptying of His previous glory, a man lowers himself by emptying himself of selfishness and pride.

> The submission of the wife neither ignores nor suppresses the liberty to which her dignity as a human person and her noble functions as a wife, mother, and companion give her the full right. . . . But it does forbid such abuse of freedom as would neglect the welfare of the family; it refuses, in this body which is the family, to allow the heart to be separated from the head, with great detriment to the body itself and even with risk of disaster. If the husband is the head of the domestic body, then the wife is its heart; and as the first hold the primacy of authority, so the second can and ought to claim the primacy of love. (*Casti Connubii*, 10)

The primacy of authority can be referred to as "charitable authority," the divinely instituted authority that is animated by *agape* love, which a husband exercises for the purpose of fostering and cultivating sanctification and full spiritual growth in his wife and children. He accomplishes this by means of his sanctification and self-donation, which is a participation in Christ's sacrifice for His Church. This vision of charitable authority is expressed succinctly by St. Paul:

> Because the husband is the head of the wife, as Christ is head of the church. He is the savior of the body.... Husbands, love your wives, as Christ also loved the church, and delivered himself up for it. (Ephesians 5:23, 25)

The fifth chapter of Ephesians provides us with the most extensive proclamation of Christian marriage in its ideal formulation contained in Scripture, while also granting men a systematic outline for exercising charitable authority as a husband in the image of Christ.

> [St. Paul presents] "the union of Christ with the Church ... under the simile of marriage, of the conjugal union of husband and wife." [In] this case, it is not merely a comparison in a metaphorical sense."

[The] "analogy of spousal or conjugal love helps to penetrate the very essence of the mystery."[165]

It should be noted that there have been attempts to soften the idea of a husband's headship by referencing the verse that precedes St. Paul's profound depiction of the vocation of marriage: "being subject one to another, in fear of Christ" (Eph 5:21).

Though these words apply to married couples, St. Paul was speaking in a universal sense to all Christians. After this verse, he proceeds to discuss what this subjection specifically looks like in the context of Christian marriage. By upholding the reality of the mutual subjection of spouses to one another, one does not deny male headship. However, to use mutual subjection as a way to dismiss the husband's headship could and would be denying the very charitable authority that fosters true mutual subjection.

This mutual subjection of spouses is the essential component of a marriage that images the love of Christ and His Church. As Pope St. John Paul points out, "To be subject to one's spouse means to be 'completely given.'"[166] In turn, mutual subjection

---

165 John Paul II, General Address 1 September, 1982.
166 Christopher West, *Theology of the Body Explained* (Boston, Massachusetts: Publisher, 2003), 51.

means a "reciprocal donation of self [when] Christ is the source and at the same time the model that subjects [it] and confers on the conjugal union a profound and mature character."[167]

Considering this, mutual subjection and authentic male headship are not mutually exclusive, but rather are interdependent upon one another. In fact, one cannot exist truly without the other. Therefore, it is imperative that we interpret St. Paul's passage on marriage through the lens of mutual submission, while upholding the essential nature and role of male headship. If we choose to deny Christian male headship, we negate mutual submission, for such submission is dependent upon proper male headship.

St. Paul's Letter to the Ephesians proposes an outline of male headship, what it reflects (Christ's headship), what constitutes it, and how a man is to live it.

St. Paul's Outline of Male Headship

The headship of a husband is depicted by St. Paul in a systematic, crafted prose. To understand the demands and responsibilities placed upon the man, it is important to also understand how St. Paul "packages" these demands within a singular idea.

Before St. Paul explains the husband's duties, he begins with an exhortation to love: "Husbands, *love* your wives, as Christ

---

167 Ibid.

also *loves* the church, and delivered himself up for it" (Eph 5:25, emphasis added). Then, in the midst of this passage—at the very heart and center—he exhorts the husband to love: "So also men ought to *love* their wives as their own bodies. He that loveth his wife, loves himself" (Eph 5:28, emphasis added). Finally, he describes the husband's responsibilities, and concludes with another exhortation to love: "Nevertheless let every one of you in particular *love* his wife as himself" (Eph 5:33, emphasis added).

The word for love that is used in each of these three occasions is a form of the Greek word *agape*, which refers to the highest form of love, or charity. The term *agape* indicates the love of God for men and of men for God. It is a universal and unconditional love that transcends and endures in all circumstances. In this sense, *agape* is distinct from *philia*, which indicates a brotherly love, or *philautia*, which is the love of self.

It appears that St. Paul purposely arranged this passage to express definitively that a man's marriage to his wife begins with love, exists with love, and loves to the end, and that this love is the love that Christ has for His Church, whom He loved even when her members were sinners.[168]

If a husband is to exercise true charitable authority, his headship must be animated by the same, unconditional love

---

168 See Rom 5:8.

with which Christ loves His Church. This places the man in a challenging and precarious position. He, by his own means, is incapable of loving his wife in the manner that Christ loved the Church. Therefore, he must humble himself as a "bride" of Christ to receive God's unconditional love that enables him to fulfill his noble call. There is no other way.

Nevertheless, true love demands that a man lead his wife and children to completion in Christ, for if he is not leading in this manner he is not loving as Christ.

Amidst this exhortation to love, St. Paul outlines three specific ways that a husband is to express *agape* to his wife as Christ loves His Church: first, He *delivered* himself for her; second, He *sanctified* her; and third, he *presented* her to God.

The spousal analogy, wherein a husband is an icon of Christ, is not a perfect representation of the man, for no man is the perfect image of Christ. Nevertheless, a husband who exercises charitable authority strives, by the grace given him, to participate in Christ's headship in these three ways.

Deliver Yourself for Her

"Husbands, love your wives, as Christ also loved the church, and delivered himself up for it" (Eph 5:25). The Greek word for deliver, *paradōken*, means to hand over, to give, or to deliver over. This is the same word that our Lord uses to describe God the Father's generosity: "If you then being evil, know how to give good gifts to your children: how much more will your Father who is in heaven, give (*paradōken*) good things to them that ask him?" (Mt 7:11).

We are to express this generosity to others as God does to us: "Give (*paradōken*) to him that asketh of thee" (Mt 5:42). Furthermore, this generosity is not limited to giving things, but also includes the sharing of one's authority as Christ shared His authority with His disciples: "And having called his twelve disciples together, he gave (*paradōken*) them power [authority] over unclean spirits" (Mt 10:1).

It appears that St. Paul's concept of a husband delivering himself to his wife is deeply rooted in the sharing of one's talents, gifts, goods, love, and authority. Such generosity grants the woman a true participation in the man's headship. This sharing (*paradōken*) of the man's authority "excludes every kind of subjection whereby a wife might become a servant or slave of the husband and an object of unilateral domination. Love makes the husband simultaneously subject to the wife and thereby to the Lord Himself, just as the wife to the husband."[169]

However, we cannot simply state that this simultaneous

---

169 John Paul II, General Audiences; *August 11, 1982.*

mutual subjection occurs without a cause or initiating force. The husband's headship mandates that he continually and consistently deliver himself to his wife for the purpose of her completion in Christ. Thus, mutual submission and a sharing of authority proceeds from the man.

Sanctify Her

"Christ [. . .] loved the church, and delivered himself up for it: that he might sanctify it, cleansing it by the laver of the water in the word of Life" (Eph 5:25–26). To be sanctified is to have the likeness of nature with the Lord. This divine likeness is only imparted by God through the Holy Spirit, particularly through the Sacrament of Baptism and the continual participation in the sacraments.

This sanctification, a work of the Holy Spirit in the human person, sets the person apart from the world, making the person, in a sense, sacred unto the Lord. Considering this, we can see that no man can sanctify his wife per se—only God can accomplish this by the infusion and impartation of grace. Nevertheless, the husband has an essential role to play in participating with Christ in His accomplishment of making his wife holy unto the Lord.

The word sanctify (in Greek, *hagios*) means sacred, holy, or to be set apart by (or for) God. Though a man cannot sanctify his wife *per se*, nevertheless he is responsible for fostering her sanctification, first, by protecting her from being assimilated into the world; second, by protecting her from his own disordered desires, particularly to objectify her sexually, or to use her as his servant; and third, by protecting her from the evil one, especially guarding her relationship with God, which includes her prayer life.

Recall that man's theological location is to stand on the horizon between the external worldly forces and the domestic garden. When a husband understands his wife to be sacred, holy, and set apart from the world, he will work tirelessly to aid her in the endeavor of protecting her feminine genius from being invaded, penetrated, or crushed under the weight of radical feminism and female rebellion.

Woman, as life-bearer, perpetuator of human life and eternal souls, must be protected and defended from a satanic culture that is bent on robbing her of her glorious vocation by removing her from the home and from her vocation of motherhood and being a wife.[170]

---

170 "While it must be recognized that women have the same right as men to perform various public functions, society must be structured in such a way that wives and mothers are not in practice compelled to work outside the home, and that their families can live and prosper in a dignified way even when they themselves

In addition to guarding her from the world, it is essential that the husband protect his wife from himself, particularly any tendencies to objectify her, or use her to satisfy his disordered passions, particularly sexual passions. Marriage never justifies lust. Lust is loosely defined as using another for one's gain, rather than sacrificing one's selfish desires for the other. Lust is not love. St. Paul is clear that male headship, if authentic, is animated by love, which aims to overcome lust in all of its forms.

Lastly, a husband is to ensure his wife's sanctification by granting her the time and space needed for consistent adoration and worship of God. Though woman is blessed with the gift of being highly relational, such gifts can subject her to the constant demands of motherhood and the cares for her husband at the neglect of attending to her prayers and devotions. It is imperative that a husband protect his wife's relationship with the Lord. By guarding her communion with God, he is nourishing his communion with her. For where the Lord is, there is love.

Finally, St. Paul associates the idea of sanctification with the

---

devote their full time to their own family. Furthermore, the mentality which honors women more for their work outside the home than for their work within the family must be overcome. This requires that men should truly esteem and love women with total respect for their personal dignity, and that society should create and develop conditions favoring work in the home." FC, 23.

cleansing bath of Baptism and the Word of life.[171] A key aspect of using one's charitable authority for the service of the wife's sanctification is the fostering of a mutual sharing of the inspirations and instructions received from God. The husband does not need to be a theologian, Bible-scholar, or an academic. Charitable authority only demands that a husband be formed by the Word of God, and that he become capable of helping form others by the transmission of the Word received. By doing this, he will become capable of transmitting God's mercy, truth, and traditions of the faith, through his word, and, more importantly, by his example.

Present Her

Lastly, the husband is not responsible for himself alone. The fact that the two are now one flesh indicates that the man not only presents himself to God in prayer and worship, but when presenting himself he presents his wife and her intentions also.

The word used for "present" contains the Greek word *histémi*, which means to make a stand, as to stand firm, to be steadfast, even in closeness. Charitable authority is characterized by a husband remaining steadfast, alongside his wife. He refuses to flee from his post. The man who is truly "head" is defined by

---

171   See Eph 5:26.

remaining at his post regardless of adversarial challenges. Adam, in silence, refrained from standing by Eve as her defense. St. Joseph initially separated himself from the situation of the Virgin Mary's pregnancy, yet returned to stand his ground as her protector. Like father, like Son, our Lord Jesus refused to flee when Judas and the cohort entered the garden to apprehend Him. He stood his ground and defended his Body of believers by laying down His very life.

Remember your wife in your prayers as another self, a completion of you, and present her to God—who dwells in both of you. If you neglect to present her to God, your presentation of yourself to God is incomplete.

The headship of a husband is essential to ensuring that your wife is protected from the world, that her dignity is fully appreciated, and that she is elevated to God in prayer. This is a tremendous responsibility, but also a most noble calling. If your headship is animated by Christ's headship, your marriage will become a living sign, a fruitful sacrament, to a world that hungers for true *agape* love.

At the heart of the renewal of all things in Christ is a marriage that is a "great sacrament; but I speak in Christ and in the church. Nevertheless, let every one of you in particular love his wife as himself: and let the wife fear her husband" (Eph 5:32–33).

CHAPTER 5

Patriarchal Authority

AT THE SERVICE OF COMPLETING THE FAMILY

To those who have been given much, much is demanded . . .

—Lk 12:48

The Stage of Manhood

As mentioned previously, the journey toward the full vision of mature manhood in Christ[172] can consist of three fundamental stages: boyhood, manhood, and fatherhood.

The stage of boyhood is defined by dependence upon superiors and progression towards personal independence from those whom the boy depends upon for his survival. It is during this

---

172 See Pt 4:13; Mature manhood consists in perfection through knowledge of Jesus Christ and the fullness of His Spirit living in us.

stage that the boy receives love and protection in hope that he becomes a man who is capable of protecting and loving others.

The boy is chiefly preoccupied with himself and the fulfillment of his passions. He is incapable of perceiving his self-centeredness and believes that the world is at his service. Because of this, he is largely incapable of seeing beyond his needs, desires, and personal, short-sighted plans. The boy only understands pain, deprivation, or suffering as something that must be avoided.

It is during this critical stage that the boy receives—or should receive—the seed of sonship, first and foremost by means of Baptism, but also by means of continual affirmation by his parents. By means of tender love, combined with consistent discipline, the boy begins to comprehend that he is a chosen son, who is made for more than fulfilling his idle passions. Unfortunately, a vast number of men never graduate from this stage and remain boys trapped in men's bodies, who are incapable of leading anyone to salvation and glory.

Enlightened by the truth that personal suffering and the sacrifice of fleeting passions are worthy and necessary for the accomplishment of a noble purpose or a desired achievement, the boy is inspired to make the transition from boyhood to manhood. By assuming responsibility for himself, the boy embarks upon the journey to manhood. He pays his debts; he labors with diligence, motivation, and excellence; and he strives for a goal or a personal purpose.

He begins to comprehend life through the lens of "purpose," which he intuits will afford him "meaning." The stage of manhood affords the man with the understanding that self-denial can lead to self-fulfillment. This self-denial often has the external appearance of solidarity with like-minded people, or with a movement, a cause, or a belief. He joins a mission, a cooperative, a business initiative, or the military, yet his chief motivation is largely to increase his capacity for personal success and exalt himself through personal achievement.

It is often, during this stage, that a man may encounter Christ and be granted the opportunity to surrender his life to the One who surrendered His life for him. Yet, if he understands the stage of manhood as his ultimate destination (his primary purpose is to be responsible for himself and his own personal fulfillment), he will inevitably twist the intention of the Gospel to be at the service of glorifying himself rather than being at the service of glorifying God.

During this stage, he realizes that personal success, and the luster of life, is not fully appreciated by living in isolation, but ought to be shared with another. This idea becomes a compelling force behind his motivations. He wants to share his life with another, and therefore he recognizes his need for another, and to be needed by another. Therefore, he considers marriage.

By means of marriage, the man unites himself to his equal, another self, a suitable partner with whom he hopes to share his dreams and future plans. Amidst the intense sentiments that are associated with being the most important person in another's life, the man rarely meditates on the profound responsibility that will be demanded of him. Yet, upon entering marriage, the man will no longer be responsible solely for himself, but for others.

Usually, not until his wife begins to bear him children, does the reality of his tremendous responsibility to defend, protect, and provide for his dependents become a primary focus and motivation in his daily decision making.

There is a grave temptation to believe that remaining in manhood is more fulfilling than the vocation of fatherhood. Manhood offers a certain quality of autonomy to the man. He is able to avoid the unforeseen suffering that is commonly associated with caring and loving others who depend upon him. Indeed, the more one loves another and is attached to another, the more acute the pain that is the consequence of witnessing the suffering of that other.

To remain in manhood, rather than proceeding to the stage of fatherhood, would be similar to a soul desiring to remain in Purgatory instead of experiencing the glory of Heaven. For after beholding the beatific vision, yet not obtaining it, Purgatory, rather than containing the hope for something greater, would become a hell, because of the loss of what it is intended to obtain. In a similar way, a man who chooses to remain in the stage of manhood, while purposefully avoiding the call to fatherhood, will become keenly aware of his personal emptiness and ever-deepening isolation.

From this point on, if the man has determined to leave the stage of boyhood irrevocably behind, he realizes that his responsibilities have multiplied exponentially. He is no longer accountable for his own well-being, but rather his cares are for the consistent and continual temporal, physical, emotional, financial, intellectual, and spiritual welfare of every member of his household—and this responsibility weighs upon him heavily. He has now entered the most demanding, purifying, and necessary stage of fatherhood.

Fatherhood is the stage of true, disinterested, masculine sacrifice. The human father embraces the daily toil of grinding labor and invests in his subjects to ensure that they each flourish—even at the cost of himself. His is a most heroic and demanding duty. The father suffers in fulfilling his responsibilities, and he suffers responsibly for his own. From this point on, responsibility and suffering are inextricably linked.

Fatherhood is divinely designed to compel the man to move from isolation to fatherhood. Yet, to do so, the man must pass through suffering, marked by personal sacrifice. Fatherhood, by its very nature, breeds communion. The father gathers his own under his care, fostering harmony by means of his disinterested love. To achieve this communion among the family it is imperative that the father overcome the desire to isolate himself with his own cares and distractions and enter the arena of suffering that is marked by personal self-donation, thus achieving the glorious crown of fatherhood.[173]

This man is the *pater familias*, the father of the family who is "over his household,"[174] whose dictum can be summed up in the phrase "as for me and my house we will serve the Lord" (Jos 24:15).

The *pater familias* is the bedrock of humanity. He is the societal, cultural, familial link that has the noble responsibility to transmit and transfer authority, kingship, heritage, and tradition to his own. Fatherhood has been divinely created to thread humanity into a unified tapestry. Yet, as grand as all of this may be, still greater and more vital is the human father's divinely

---

173 See Karol Wojtyla, *Radiation of Fatherhood*, 1964. Wojtyla contends that Adam remained in isolation rather than progressing through the stage of suffering marked by personal sacrifice. That on the frontier between loneliness and fatherhood is suffering.

174 See Lk 12; Mt 24.

ordained mission to "relive and reveal the very fatherhood of God."[175] God names the human father in His name—Father—and appoints him to be a representation of the divine paternity.[176] To effectively accomplish this, the Lord calls him to meditate on his fatherhood by comparing it to the perfect fatherhood of God.[177]

It has been argued that human fatherhood, by its negligence, tyranny, and misuse and abuse of its authority, has disfigured (from the human perspective) the image of God's fatherhood. However, the influence and power of fatherhood, the *via negativa*, testifies to the potential and power of the *pater familias*—and its unique ability to be a link between God and man. In other words, if a human father, by his bad actions can mar the image of God the Father, how much more powerfully can he, by his good actions, image God the Father's goodness. Indeed, the vocation of fatherhood is designed in such a way to be a link between the divine Father and families.

---

175 *FC*, 25.

176 "For this cause I bow my knees to the Father of our Lord Jesus Christ, of whom all paternity in heaven and earth is named." Eph 3:14–15.

177 "If you then being evil know how to give good gifts to your children: how much more will your Father who is in heaven, give good things to them that ask him?" Mt 7:11; Our Lord asks us to compare our desire for our children to be enriched with blessings, with our heavenly Father who always desires that which is greatest for us. By meditating upon how we desire our children to succeed, to have good health, in a word, to have a bountiful fulfilled life, we comprehend, even a glimpse of the unlimited generosity, benevolence and love God the Father has for us.

This is precisely the reason that human fatherhood is degraded, demeaned, vehemently opposed, subversively attacked, demoralized, and disregarded as an antiquated, useless form of male tyranny that simply needs to step aside for the sake of cultural "advancements" and societal "developments."

Indeed, the evil one is keenly aware that if he is to successfully destroy the Church, he must crush, redefine, and malign the family (the domestic church); and to penetrate and subdue the family, it is essential that he sideline and spiritually paralyze and restrain the human father from accomplishing his divinely instituted mission.

This satanic agenda became explicitly embodied by the radical feminist revolution that launched in the United States during the late 1960s. A prominent founding figure of the radical feminist movement began her gatherings with the following mantra:

Why are we here today? To make revolution. What kind of revolution? The cultural revolution. How do we make cultural revolution? By destroying the American family. How do we destroy the family? By destroying the American patriarch. How do we destroy the American patriarch? By taking away his power. How do we destroy his power? By destroying monogamy. How do we destroy monogamy? By promoting promiscuity, eroticism, prostitution and homosexuality.[178]

The human father, though often obliviously unaware, is at the center of a cosmic battle between the forces of good and evil, which the French poet Charles Peguy aptly describes:

> There is only one adventurer in the world . . . the father of a family. Even the most desperate adventurers are nothing compared to him. Everything is against him. Savagely organized against him. Everything turns and combines against him. . . . Everything is against the father of a family, the *Pater Familias*; and consequently against the family. He alone is literally "engaged" in the world, in the age. He alone is an adventurer.[179]

My brother, we must not deem such statements as exaggerative or hyperbolic, nor should words such as these astonish us.

---

178 Quoted by Piers Shepherd, *The Catholic World Report*, online edition, "Expert on Marriage and Family: The Father-Son Bond Is 'Civilization's Keystone,'" www.catholicworldreport.com/2019/05/08/the-father-son-bond-as-civilizations-keystone/, accessed 3/19/2020.

179 Charles Peguy, 1908.

Sacred Scripture attests to the vitality, necessity, and divinely instituted mission of fatherhood:

> He shall turn the heart of fathers to their children
> and the heart of children to their fathers: lest I come
> and strike the earth with anathema. (Malachi 4:6)

God, through the prophet Malachi, revealed that the human father is fundamental to God's mission to save the world from damnation and disaster. Indeed, the prophetic oracle contains within itself both a warning and a remedy. The warning is that if fathers do not turn their hearts toward their children, then children will eventually learn to distrust their fathers and neglect to turn to their fathers with trust. If this occurs, which is precisely what is taking place in our age, God will allow the inhabitants of the earth to endure His curse.

The word anathema literally means to be excommunicated or to be cast out. In other words, by neglecting the responsibility to love their children and raise them in the ways of the Lord, fathers are inadvertently excommunicating their children from communion with God the Father, while also excommunicating themselves from God and their own children.

Why is God's warning so severe? When children distrust the

love of their human fathers, who are supposed to be a human representation of the divine Father, they learn to distrust God the Father. Children of negligent fathers will teach their children to neglect their heavenly Father, and eventually humanity will no longer seek the loving gaze and protection of God the Father but turn to idols instead.

Yet, contained within this prophecy is also a solution: when the human father loves his child with the love that he has received from God his father, his child will not only trust in his earthly father's love, but, more importantly, the child will learn to trust and embrace his heavenly Father's love.

Sons who trust in God the Father will become fathers who raise trusting sons, and it is men such as these who will restore and revitalize the Kingdom of God on earth. This ordinary means of perpetuating the Gospel and transmitting belief in Jesus Christ is expressed figuratively by St. John the Evangelist in his recounting of the historical event of the healing of the royal official's son.

Recall that our Lord's first public miracle at the Wedding of Cana, recounted by St. John, was His apparent confirmation of his restoration and redemption of human marriage. In addition to this, St. John notes that the second of our Lord Jesus' public miracles was the healing of the royal official's son. This miracle occurred when:

> He came again therefore into Cana of Galilee, where he made the water wine. And there was a certain ruler, whose son was sick at Capharnaum. He having heard that Jesus was come from Judea into Galilee, went to him, and prayed him to come down, and heal his son; for he was at the point of death. Jesus therefore said to him: Unless you see signs and wonders, you believe not. The ruler saith to him: Lord, come down before that my son die. Jesus saith to him: Go thy way; thy son liveth. The man believed the word which Jesus said to him and went his way. And as he was going down, his servants met him; and they brought word, saying, that his son lived. He asked therefore of them the hour wherein he grew better. And they said to him: Yesterday at the seventh hour, the fever left him. The father therefore knew that it was at the same hour that Jesus said to him, Thy son liveth; and himself believed, and his whole house. This is again the second miracle that Jesus did, when he was come out of Judea into Galilee. (John 4:46–53)

If our Lord Jesus' first public miracle, which occurred on the "seventh day," was a sign of His desire to heal, redeem, and sacramentalize marriage, it also seems that the evangelist is conveying that Christ's second public miracle, which occurred at the seventh hour, is a certain sign of His intention to restore and redeem the relationship between the human father and his child.[180] The seventh hour is a vivid symbol of a new beginning for human fatherhood, which by Christ's incarnation, has the power to "relive and reveal the fatherhood of God."[181]

It appears that the evangelist, by the recounting of Christ's first two public miracles, is demonstrating the ordinary means by which Christ desires to save the world: marriage and the family. This is a reasonable conclusion when we consider that Sr. Lucia, who as a young child witnessed the apparitions of Our Lady of Fatima, said, "The last battle between God and Satan

---

180 This account combined with the fact that after the transfiguration of Christ in both Mark and Matthew, which is a pre-figuration of His resurrection, Christ is asked by his disciples why the scribes say that Elijah has to come before the Messiah. Jesus reveals that Elijah did come in the person of St. John the Baptist who "Shall go in the spirit and power Elijah to turn the hearts of fathers to children and the incredulous to the wisdom of the just, to prepare a perfect people" (Mt 17). Then immediately after saying this, Jesus' first miracle is the deliverance of a boy possessed by a demon at the incessant request of his father. It seems that both Matthew and Mark, by connecting the prophecy from Malachi with the immediate action of driving out a demon that separates a father and son, the Gospel writers are hinting at the ordinary means of the perpetuating of the Gospel: Fathers turn your hearts toward your children.

181 See *FC*, 25.

will be over the family and marriage." Indeed, the human father is being summoned to the front lines of this epic battle.

My brother, you and your fatherhood are indispensable to the propagation of the Gospel and the re-building of the Church. This is supported by St. John's concluding remarks regarding Christ's second public miracle: "And himself [the royal official] believed, and his whole family" (Jn 4:53). In other words, when a father surrenders his life to Christ, his family ordinarily follows his example.

Peppered throughout the New Testament is the re-occurring theme of the *pater familias*, who after becoming a believer in Christ, his entire household follows his example.[182]

As with male-headship, fatherhood has at best become a lost art and, at worst, has been reduced to a meaningless, ineffective, unneeded role. Yet, fatherhood, as proven statistically,[183] is vital, essential, and necessary for the restoration of the family, the revitalization of the Church, and the conversion of the world. The vocation of fatherhood and the winning of souls for Christ are inextricably connected.

If manhood culminates in spiritual fatherhood, and the fulfillment of masculinity is spiritual paternity, it is essential that the divinely instituted vocation of spiritual fatherhood be

---

182 See Acts 16:25–40; 10:36–48.
183 See *Show Us the Father*, Devin Schadt; Totus Tuus Press, 2016.

recovered and re-discovered with new zeal. It is crucial that the human father understand that he is called to be a living icon of the Heavenly Father.

Head of His House

The culminating stage of the masculine journey is the vocation of the *pater familias*, the father of the family, which can never be reduced to being a passive figurehead or a mere biological reality. A symbol of strength, fidelity, solidarity, stability, experiential wisdom, and unity, the *pater familias* is the head around which the body of his family is gathered, and by whom they are gathered into the Lord.

As he ages, his wisdom should deepen. His sound counsel imparts the wisdom that helps his family respond to and navigate the riddles and perplexities of life. Even if his children and children's children seek not his counsel directly, he stands as a visible anchor that remains unmoved amidst the world's violent storms. By his stalwart presence and unshakable faith, the members of his household are inspired to persevere in the face of the unknown and unpredictable. His fortitude reassures his family that despite trials and tribulations it is possible to remain faithful to God.

It is for this reason that the devil wages war on the *pater familias*. The evil one is very aware that if the father is removed from his office of being over his household, or if he misuses or abuses this office, the members of his house will become disheartened and often disband.

Indeed, the *pater familias* holds an essential position in the plan of salvation. He is at the center of the conversion of worldly souls for he, unlike the priest, lives in both the sacred and secular spheres. He therefore has the unique responsibility of drawing men from the world to the priest, and ultimately to God. Yet, he must avoid being drawn into the world's seductions, and, because of this, his location between the world and the family is continually under fire.

His life is to be a witness of the power of God's transformative love and grace. He is vital to the renewal of the universal Church and the restoration of the domestic church, the family, which comprises the universal Church, and, therefore, he is foundational to the renewal of all things in Christ.

The concept of *pater familias*, Latin for "father of the family" or "owner of the family estate," was the head of a Roman family. The *pater familias* was normally the oldest male in the home, and he exercised authority over the entire family.

Though the Romans coined the term *pater familias*, the concept of a man having authority over his house is evident in the most ancient societies and is mentioned in several scriptural accounts such as in the case of Joseph, the son of Jacob, who was placed over the house of Pharaoh;[184] and Shebna,[185] who over the household of the King of Israel. The Hebrew title for over the house, ʿal- hab-bā-yiṭ, is an official office. The ʿal- hab-bā-yiṭ is the respected position of the steward who has been given authority over his master's house, which includes being a father to the master's subjects.

Though the ʿal- hab-bā-yiṭ, or master of the household, was intended to be a virtuous form of governance and sodality, ensuring harmony, peace, and provision, it was often, as demonstrated in the ancient Roman culture, abused and corrupted by the desire for power. This perversion marked by tyranny has forever haunted the human father whose authority is continually misunderstood as being domineering and despotic. Indeed, when the steward loses touch with the reality that he is ultimately at the service of his household, his authority becomes disordered, and his rule revolted against. Consequently, those

---

184 "Thou shalt be over my house, and at the commandment of thy mouth all the people shall obey: only in the kingly throne will I be above thee." Gn 41:40.

185 "Thus saith the Lord God of hosts: Go, get thee in to him that dwelleth in the tabernacle, to Sobna who is over the temple: and thou shalt say to him." Is 22:14.

who attempt to assume their office of fatherly authority are gravely misunderstood.

The evil one's methodology is to distort the meaning of something that is originally good, so that it represents something evil. Then, after the devil has convinced people to associate that original good with being evil, he sides with these truth seekers, supporting and encouraging them in their conviction that the original good is bad. By doing so, he distances the human being from the truth and from God, and from God's original intentions for the good. This demonic dynamic applies in a particular way to the *pater familias*.

Rather than dismissing, removing, or destroying a cultural custom, our Lord redeems it by giving it the meaning with which it was originally created. For example, the Pharisees pressed Jesus on the question of divorce based on their distorted and misunderstood view of marriage. Rather than dismissing marriage for the disfigured version it has become, our Lord reminded His questioners of God's original intention when He created the union of man and woman.[186]

In a similar way, our Lord does not dismiss the reality and vitality of the *pater familias* because of those who have abused

---

186 See Mt 19:8.

its power and authority, but rather He offers the glorious and redeemed vision of this most necessary office.

Christ's Pattern of the *Pater Familias*

The concept of the *pater familias* is mentioned on a number of occasions in the New Testament. The majority of these occurrences—if not all—are spoken by our Lord Jesus himself, who used this term in many of His parables.[187] The Greek word for *pater familias*, *oikodespotes*, is only uttered by Christ himself and is often translated as "over the household," or more literally "head of the house." In other words, the *pater familias* is the father of the family who exercises headship (authority) over his household.

The fact that this phrase is used exclusively by our Lord grants it a heightened significance. Our Lord seems to be indicating that the properly defined version of the *pater familias*, the head of the house, originates from and is fulfilled by Him.

Our Lord Jesus outlines the tremendous responsibility of the head of the house with acute clarity in two very similar accounts.[188]

> But this know ye, that if the householder did know
> at what hour the thief would come, he would surely

---

187 See Mt 10:25; 13:27, 52; 20:1, 11; 21:33; 24:43; Mk 14;4; Lk 12:39; 13:25; 14:21; 22:11.
188 See Lk 12:24; Mt 24:43.

watch, and would not suffer his house to be broken open. Be you then also ready: for at what hour you think not the Son of man will come. And Peter said to him: Lord, dost thou speak this parable to us, or likewise to all? And the Lord said: Who (thinkest thou) is the faithful and wise steward, whom his lord setteth over his family, to give them their measure of wheat in due season? Blessed is that servant whom, when his lord shall come, he shall find so doing. Verily I say to you, he will set him over all that he possesseth. But if that servant shall say in his heart: My Lord is long a coming; and shall begin to strike the men-servants and maid-servants, and to eat and to drink and be drunk: The lord of that servant will come in the day that he hopeth not, and at the hour that he knoweth not: and shall separate him and shall appoint him his portion with unbelievers. And that servant, who knew the will of his lord and prepared not himself and did not according to his will, shall be beaten with many stripes. But he that knew not and did things worthy of stripes shall be beaten with few stripes. And unto whomsoever much is given, of him much shall be required:

and to whom they have committed much, of him they will demand the more. (Luke 12:39–48)

In this passage, our Lord succinctly outlines the major characteristics of the *pater familias*: first, he has authority over his family as indicated by phrases "householder" and "setteth over his family." Second, his authority is given by another. This indicates that he is responsible to God who grants him the authority to be the "householder" and "steward" over his family as demonstrated by the phrase "And unto whomsoever much is given, of him much will be required." Third, he has been charged with the mission to protect his household as indicated by the phrase "He would surely watch and not allow his home to be broken open." Fourth, he is given the duty to provide for his family as indicated by the phrase "to give them their measure of wheat in due season." Fifth, he is to be the "priest" of his family as indicated by the words "faithful and wise steward." The father-priest transmits God's teaching to his family and confirms these teachings by his self-donation and prudential example. Sixth, he is the servant of both the master from whom he derives his authority and also the servant of his subjects, as indicated by the phrases "blessed is that servant," "if that servant shall say in his heart," and "the Lord of that servant." Seventh, he is not to misuse or abuse his authority as indicated by Christ's reprimand of the neglectful householder who "begins to strike the menservants and maid servants, and to eat and drink and be drunk."

The *pater familias* receives his authority from God and is responsible to God for being the protector, provider, and the priest of his family. By fulfilling this duty, he becomes a true servant of God and his family. Such a man glorifies God and thus is glorified by God.

The Enemy of the *Pater Familias*

As protector, provider, and priest of his household, the *pater familias* is of central importance to the divine mission of saving souls, and because of this he will consistently be enmeshed in spiritual combat.

Therefore, it is not sufficient for the head of the house to understand that his objective is the salvation of the members of his household, including himself. It is imperative also that he understand his enemy's purpose, comprehending to some degree his diabolic strategy, lest he be deposed, and his family plundered.

The enemy of course is the devil, the "a liar, and the father thereof," "the murderer from the beginning,"[189] the "tempter,"[190]

---

189 Ibid.
190 Mt 4:3.

the "prince of demons,"[191] the "ruler of darkness,"[192] "the god of this world,"[193] "the old serpent, which is the devil and Satan,"[194] "Lucifer, the son of morning,"[195] and the "wicked one,"[196] who is "your adversary."[197]

My brother, it is imperative that you be aware and believe that "our wrestling is not against flesh and blood; but against principalities and power, against the rulers of the world of this darkness, against the spirits of wickedness in high places. " (Eph 6:12).

Drawing heavily upon St. Thomas Aquinas, we will succinctly describe the method and motivations behind the devil's strategy and how he works to penetrate the deep recesses of man's heart for the purpose of binding him in spiritual paralysis, fear, addiction, and lukewarmness to disarm him from being a threat to his demonic dominion. We will outline, first, the two sins of the devil and his demons; second, the two purposes of the devil; third, the two causes of man sinning; fourth, the two paths the devil uses to slither sin into man's soul; fifth, the two ways by

---

191 Lk 11:15; Mk 3:22; Mt 9:34.
192 See Eph 6:12.
193 2 Cor 4:4.
194 Rev 20:2.
195 See Is 14:12.
196 1 Jn 2:13.
197 1 Pt 5:8.

which he accomplishes this demonic penetration of man's soul; and sixth, the two chief instruments the evil one uses to bind the man from excelling as the *pater familias*.

The Sins and Purposes of the Devil

According to St. Thomas, the devil and demons are fallen angels who, though they lead man to commit every type of sin, they themselves, being purely spiritual (that is they don't possess physical bodies), do not have a tendency toward the sins of the flesh, but rather sin in two ways: pride and envy.[198]

The devil commits the sin of pride. He desires to be like God, or to be as God. He attempts "to achieve his own final beatitude without God's assistance and aid, and to have command over others in a way proper to God alone."[199]

The evil one cannot—in his desire to be like God, or in his pursuit to have the ultimate power of God—ever achieve true beatitude for only true beatitude is in God and imparted by God, who is the beatific vision that grants eternal fulfillment and lasting joy.

This impediment eternally frustrates and infuriates the devil, filling him with the most intense and insidious malice. En-

---

198 The Catholic Thing, "Aquinas on Demons" (September 19, 2016), www.thecatholicthing.org/2016/09/19/aquinas-on-demons/, accessed 3/19/2020.
199 Ibid.

raged by this hatred, he becomes envious of God and also those to whom God is drawing, or has drawn, into full and final beatitude.

"Envy is sorrow for another's good,"[200] "in so far as it conduces to the lessening of one's own good name or excellence. It is in this way that envy grieves for another's good: and consequently, men are envious of those goods in which a good name consists, and about which men like to be honored and esteemed."[201] "So, after the sin of pride, there follows the evil of envy in the sinning angel, whereby he grieves over man's good, and also over the divine excellence, according as against the devil's will God makes use of man for the divine glory."[202]

Therefore, "by the envy of the devil, death came into the world" (Wis 2:24). Misery wants company, therefore, the devil—out of envy for God and those to whom God imparts his grace—strives to ensure that mankind never experiences the supreme bliss, joy, and peace of God's eternal beatitude.

It is from the devil's two main sins (pride and envy) that his two chief purposes arise: first, to wage war incessantly upon man for the purpose of thwarting his salvation and hindering his spiritual progress; and second, to torture the damned. The

---

200 St. Thomas Aquinas, *Summa Theologiae: Envy (Secunda Secundae Partis)*, Q. 36).
201 Ibid.
202 St. Thomas Aquinas, *Summa Theologiae: Envy (Secunda Secundae Partis)*, Q 63.

evil one attempts to be God by claiming souls for himself, compelling the damned souls to curse God rather than praise Him.

By achieving these two purposes, the devil aspires to build a kingdom that is more expansive than God's.

The devil is not concerned as much with owning persons in particular, but rather enslaving entire populaces. The evil one does not desire individuals as much as a quantity of souls. Sleeplessly, he crafts and schemes for the purpose of deceiving and addicting a numberless ocean of souls into his vast, hopeless, inescapable Hell.

You are his chief target because you are a human image of the eternal Father, a link between God and man. Though you may be important in the plan of God, the devil views you as another soon to be forgotten, nameless soul, another splice of humanity added to his pyre of plunder, and fuel to be consumed, yet never fully consumed by his eternal malice.

The Two Causes of Sin

In his notable parable regarding the householder and the thief, the Lord warns us, "If the householder did know at what hour the thief would come, he would surely watch, and would not suffer his house to be broken open" (Lk 12:39).

The thief that our Lord Jesus speaks of is certainly a figure of Himself, the good thief who comes to ransom souls that Satan has stolen from God the Father. However, our Lord also is referring to the householder, the father of the family, and warning him to be on guard against the thief, the devil, who comes "to steal, ant to kill, and to destroy" (Jn 10:10).

Our Lord is He who leads all captivity (those bound to the devil) captive (free in Christ united to the Father).[203] Indeed, Christ is the ultimate good thief who takes back that which is rightfully his, that which the devil has stolen—the souls of mankind. Jesus warns the householder to beware of the devil who comes to steal his family's faith, kill their souls, and destroy their hope for Heaven. You, my brother, stand in between your family and the devil; therefore, he will do all in his power to disarm you.

The devil, however, cannot force or compel a person to sin. Considering this, we can conclude that the devil is not the only cause of sin. Indeed, there exist two causes of sin: the devil and a person's misuse of his own free will.

The devil is always the primary, indirect cause of sin, as exemplified by the Fall of man. Man's free will is the direct, secondary cause. Man alone is ultimately responsible for himself, his actions, and his sin. Again, the devil cannot move or compel your will—only you and God can operate your will. Fortunately,

---

203 "Wherefore he saith: Ascending on high, he led captivity captive; he gave gifts to men." Eph 4:8.

"charity in the slightest degree is able to resist sin."[204] As St. Peter says, "Charity covereth a multitude of sins" (1 Pt 4:8). Therefore, if we use our free will to extend even the slightest act of charity toward God or our neighbor, the devil will be overcome.

My brother, your free will, operated and influenced by right reason, enables you to rise above temptation. This is the reason why a well-informed conscience is necessary. A man must be informed by God and, therefore, submit himself to the authorities that God has established, namely the Church. He is to use his intellect to choose the good and perform an act of love, rather than submit to the slavery of sin.

The *pater familias*, by depending upon God, becomes the faithful and wise servant; that is, he is faithful to God by exercising prudence in choosing the good rather than evil.

An active, informed conscience is the gate that allows the good to enter the soul of man and, eventually, that of his family. At times, this gate must be barred to keep evil from penetrating his household.

Satan's Two Path's to the Soul

My brother, the devil will attempt to bypass your intellect and slither his way into your soul by two pathways: your imagi-

---

204 Ibid.

nation and your appetite. The evil one attempts to move and sway your imagination. By means of diabolical suggestions, he attempts to awaken your appetite to desire the suggested object. In other words, the evil one darkens the intellect by appealing to your imagination (suggestions that are against the good) and then uses sensitive appetites to appeal to that imagination so that one desires to obtain that which the devil suggests.

For example, the evil one suggests to a man the idea of a female co-worker being attracted to him. By engaging that suggestion in his imagination, he begins to consider what he imagines. Initially, the thought appears to be fleeting, almost unnoticeable, having the appearance of harmlessness like a light breeze that passes quickly. Yet, the devil, seeing that the man did not reject the suggestions, continues to re-present the idea to his imagination until his appetite for lust and sexual intercourse with her are awakened.

If the man pursues the object that has been proposed to him, or if he becomes persuaded to act upon the temptation, he has sinned, and this act was committed not directly by the devil, but rather by means of the man's free will.

The devil, as the primary indirect cause, persuaded the man by means of his imagination and awakened his appetite to commit the sin by enticing the man to activate his free will against right reason.

After the appetite is awakened, the devil will approach the man's intellect with reasons or arguments that justify the sin as being good. For example, in the above-mentioned case, the devil might suggest to the man that adultery with his co-worker is acceptable because his wife no longer loves him, or that his wife has made his life unbearable and that no man should live his life unloved. The evil one usually approaches those who have some level of commitment to God by suggesting that the sin is justifiable.

Once the act is committed, the devil will turn on the man, convicting him of his guilt, and then suggest to him that God will not forgive him. If the man does not turn to God in trust and repentance, then either the man will despair of his transgression, or, more likely, the devil will continue to agitate the man's appetite, seducing him to hunger for more of the same sin until he becomes steeped in addictive behavior. When dependence upon the sin has been solidified, the devil's deception becomes man's addiction.

Let us return to the example of the man who has allowed his reason to be bypassed, his imagination manipulated, and his disordered appetites awakened by the thought of engaging his co-worker in adultery. After he has been lured to the very edge of the precipice of sin, he attempts to act upon what he has imagined, but the woman rejects him. To console himself and feed the already awakened appetite, he uses another method to indulge his lusts, such as pornography, or even engaging a less attractive woman. Afterward, he repeatedly returns to feed the appetite, which will always be hungry for more, and thereby he becomes addicted to the sinful behavior.

This grants us an important insight into the devil's methodology: he may spend much time, perhaps even years and decades, attempting to awaken certain appetites in the man, so that when even the slightest temptation occurs, the man falls without any fight.

Men are often surprised by their own lack of self-control and inability to master their passions in the moment of temptation, believing that they were suddenly ambushed by Satan. Yet, the reality is that the devil and his demons had been systematically grinding down the man's ability to reason correctly for some time, preparing him for this instantaneous disaster.

Satan's Strategy to Overthrow the *Pater Familias*

Consider that the devil's desire is to devour and destroy the woman and the child[205] and "to make war with the rest of

---

her seed, who keep the commandments of God, and have the testimony of Jesus Christ" (Rev 12:17). His intent is to destroy, malign, and redefine the family, twisting its image so that it no longer reflects the self-giving love of the Trinity. It is the *pater familias* who must keep watch to ensure that the thief does not enter his house and plunder his greatest goods.

The evil one and his demons do not know, and cannot know, the internal dispositions, thoughts, and sentiments of a man. However, the demonic forces test men from the outside for the purpose of gaining knowledge of their internal dispositions, which helps them identify the man's weakness and what will cause him to fall.

This trial of temptation is the evil one's way of testing the man to determine what he is made of. The devil "explores the inward disposition of man so that he may tempt him to that vice to which he is most prone."[206] The two primary instruments that the devil uses during his exploration of the interior man are the flesh and the world: particularly worldly advantages and persecutions.

The evil one will continually, relentlessly test and try the man for the purpose of determining which fleshly desires he is unwilling to resist. By means of these temptations, the devil consistently hammers on the man, weakening his will, and

206 St. Thomas, *Summa Theologiae*: First Part, Q. 114)

enslaving him to sin for the purpose of rendering him incapable of leading his family to God.

The devil's chief purpose is to use the weaknesses of the man in order to debilitate and incapacitate his fatherhood from being an open channel of God's grace and life for his family. If a man be bound by lust, how can he teach his daughters to avoid lustful men? If a man be intemperate, how can he summon his children to moderation? If a man be slothful, how will his children learn to love a disciplined life and learn to persevere in the face of adversity?

If the head of the house cannot protect himself, how can he defend the members of his house? If the thief has robbed the householder of his virtue, how can he stop the devil from binding his family in vice? Indeed, if the gate of his soul is breeched by evil, evil will enter and consume his house.

Besides using the flesh, the devil will test the *pater familias* to determine if he can resist worldly advantages and overcome persecution and adversity. Indeed, worldly advantages and persecution are intrinsically linked.

The more that the provider obtains and accumulates by means of worldly advantage, the greater is his attachment to such worldly forces. He who pays the piper picks the tune, and, when a man receives worldly advantages by means of a human source, he will be subject to that provider's dictates.

The receiver of worldly advantages does not immediately perceive his position as enslavement, for the devil does not demand, immediately, that the man deny God, his faith, his morals, or his beliefs. Rather, the evil one allows time to pass, which solidifies the man's dependence upon worldly favors. When the householder becomes dependent upon such favors, he orders his life, his labors, and his spending around the purpose of protecting that which he has obtained.

Such a man convinces himself that he must protect his worldly position, his relationships, and his goods, lest he lose these benefits and his situation be lost. Ironically, by focusing his efforts on not losing his possessions, or those relationships that bring him advantage, he risks losing his greatest "possession," which is his family and their salvation.

This dynamic is exacerbated and becomes increasingly evident when persecution or adversity demands the surrender of worldly goods. Often the householder who is attached to his worldly advantages, after being faced with the choice of separating himself from the world's favors for the sake of remaining faithful to God, becomes compromised.

One of the most telling tests that the *pater familias* will encounter in his duty to provide for his family is the ultimatum to surrender or compromise his beliefs in exchange for keeping, maintaining, or gaining worldly honor, favors, and acceptance by men.

Yet, even if the father of the house is able to avoid sins such as these, the devil will not delay long before returning with perhaps greater temptations.

Consider, again, that the fallen angels do not sin in the flesh for they are not corporal beings. Their sins consist of either pride or envy, if not always both. As you progress spiritually, and the Lord provides you with the grace to conquer and overcome the flesh and its disordered appetites, the devil will assail you with severe temptations to commit sins of pride and envy.

Indeed, the holier that you become, the more you will comprehend the grave and despicable nature of pride and envy. The *pater familias* will be tempted to misuse his power and authority to be "like God," attempting to glorify himself by using God for his own personal glory. There are those who serve God for his glory, and there are those who believe God is to serve them for their own glory. In the end, only one will be glorified, and, ultimately, it is not the man who glorifies himself.

My brother, a way to continually test yourself for the purpose of determining whether you are a man who desires to be "a god," or a man who desires to serve God, is by assessing whether you are pleased at another's success, goodness, and glory—especially when you had no part in their blessing, or you lack that particular blessing. The man who is thankful to God for His goodness and grace in others—without being sorrowful for what he seems to lack—is truly capable of exercising authority. Such a man will use his authority to build others up in Christ rather than puffing himself up in the name of Christ.

Now that we have considered the devil and our personal enemy, which is the misuse of our own free will, let us meditate upon the examples of Adam, the father of our race, his typological fulfillment St. Joseph, who the Church identifies as the "wise and prudent servant placed over his master's household,"[207] and his ultimate typological fulfillment, the New and Final Adam, Jesus Christ, who is the definitive ruler "over the house of Jacob,"[208] and discover how to, and how not to, embrace and exercise the role and responsibility of the *pater familias*, which is a vocation certainly inclined toward sainthood.

Adam's Dominion

The theme of God entrusting man with the task to reign and bring order to that with which he has been entrusted can be traced to the very beginnings of man, indeed the earliest

---

207 *Roman Missal,* March 19.
208 See Lk 1:31; Heb 3.

scriptural accounts. The sacred writers of the two creation accounts relate that God granted Adam dominion over creation saying, "Let him have dominion over the fishes of the sea, and the fowls of the air, and the beasts, and the whole earth, and every creeping creature that moveth upon the earth" (Gn 1:26).

Several verses later, God gave the first virgin couple the mission to rule. "And God blessed them, saying: Increase and multiply, and fill the earth, and subdue it, and rule over the fishes of the sea, and the fowls of the air, and all living creatures that move upon the earth" (Gn 1:28).

Prior to blessing the first couple (as expressed in the first creation account), the second creation account explains that God commanded Adam with instructions prior to Eve's existence, implying that his was the task to communicate the divine commands to Eve after her creation. This responsibility to transmit the divine ordinances is a priestly function because of its fidelity to God by teaching and living God's commands, which are at the service of salvation.

The Hebrew word for dominion, *radah*,[209] means to reign, or pre vail against.[210] In the person of Adam, we are afforded the original

---

209 Used in both Genesis 1:26 and Genesis 1:28.

210 See *radah*. Bible Tools, www.bibletools.org/index.cfm/fuseaction/Lexicon.show/ID/H7287/radah.htm, accessed 3/19/2020.

prototype of the *oikodespotes*, who was given the duty to prevail against an enemy by, first, protecting his domain; second, providing for himself and his subjects; and third, fulfilling his priestly office by communicating and living the commands of God.

In the original man, we see the basic characteristics of the *pater familias* that are outlined in greater detail by Christ in his parables, a framework that conveys man's tremendous responsibility before God.[211]

> It is part of God's design that human beings should have dominion over other created things (represented here by the animals). This dominion makes man God's representative (everything really belongs to God) in the created world. Therefore, although man is going to be the lord of creation, he needs to recognize that God alone is the Creator; man has to respect and look after creation; he is responsible for it.[212]

This sacred responsibility also includes Adam's respect of, care for, and protection of his wife, whom he "called woman, because she was taken out of man" (Gn 2:23), and who "Adam

---

211 See Lk 12.
212 *Navarre Bible*, Commentary Genesis Chapter 1:27, p 42.

called the name of his wife Eve: because she was mother of all the living" (Gn 3:20).

The naming of Eve does not indicate that Adam has dominion over his wife as he does over other created things, but it does demonstrate his responsibility for her. Indeed, as St. Ambrose wrote, "You are not her master, but her husband; she was not given to you to be your slave, but your wife. . . . Reciprocate her attentiveness to you and be grateful to her for her love."[213]

The Hebrew tradition of naming another implies that the person who names another is claiming that person as his own. Christ Himself renames several of his Apostles as a sign of his claiming them as his own.[214] Yet, there is an important and essential distinction between claiming ownership over another and claiming responsibility for another. A man should not attempt to own his wife in the way that one owns an object, but rather he is to claim responsibility for his wife as though she were his own soul.[215]

A husband is always responsible to God the Creator first and the creature, including his wife, second. By serving the creature, he serves the Creator, and, by assuming responsibility for the creature, he becomes responsible to the Creator.

---

213 FC, 25.

214 Jesus renames Simon as Peter; Christ renames Saul as Paul.

215 "So also ought men to love their wives as their own bodies. He that loveth his wife loveth himself." Eph 5:28.

If a husband loves his wife over and above God, he "loves" the creature above the Creator, and she that was intended to be a link to God becomes an impediment to his soul and his salvation. Again, "[Man] needs to recognize God alone is Creator,[216] man has to respect and look after creation; he is responsible for it."[217]

Regarding his relationship to his wife, man sins in two general ways: first, he can attempt to make her a slave to his own passions and desires, or, alternately, he can become enslaved to his wife and her passions and desires. In both of these circumstances, the woman becomes an obstacle to the man's vocation as head of his household. Indeed, "a house divided against itself cannot stand."[218]

Adam's chief failure consisted in that he did not fulfill the divine command to protect his domain, but rather allowed the serpent, the devil, to have unchecked access to his wife, thus exposing her to the shame of sin.[219]

After the devil seduced Eve, Eve then tempted Adam, who was with her.[220] It seems that the evil one was aware that if he

---

216 *Navarre Bible*, Commentary Genesis Chapter 1:27, p 42.

217 *Navarre Bible*, Commentary Genesis Chapter 1:27, p 42.

218 See Mk 3:25.

219 See Gen 3.

220 "And the woman saw that the tree was good to eat, and fair to the eyes, and delightful to behold: and she took of the fruit thereof, and did eat, and gave to

approached Adam first, he would not have been able to convince Adam to sin. Instead, the devil used that which Adam loved against him.

How difficult it must have been for Adam to overcome the temptation to partake of the forbidden fruit when it was proposed to him by his lover and not his enemy. Adam was confronted with the demand to be faithful to God at the risk of straining his relationship with his wife. Adam, who was bound to his wife by love, allowed that love to become a poisonous type of lust. Indeed, he refused to deny her for fear of losing her, and, therefore, by lusting for her affection, he compromised her love.

How often does a husband cave on moral issues in relationship to his wife and children due to a fear of straining his relationship with them—particularly in the sphere of sexual morality. This indeed is a grave temptation. Often, the father-leader is fooled into believing that standing firm to his moral principles he will risk isolation from his loved ones.

Adam's sin is essentially that he allowed Eve, his wife, to subdue his authority. Indeed, the hierarchal order of sacrificial responsibility became usurped by Eve, enabling her to bypass

---

her husband who did eat." Gn 3:6; The sacred text appears to imply that Adam was present in abdicative silence.

Adam's authority, which ultimately made him and his descendant's slaves to the devil.

Adam did not exercise dominion (*radah*), that is, "to reign and prevail against" the devil. To prevail over the devil, he would have had to prevail over Eve and her ambition "to be like God."

Considering these insights, we can interpret God's curse upon the woman, "Thou shalt be under thy husband's power, and he shall have dominion over thee" (Gen 3:16.), as a punishment and a remedy. Indeed, the Lord does not discipline except to bring about repentance. Punishment, as a form of discipline, is applied for the purpose of teaching the disciple how to follow Christ.

The divine "curse" is a remedy because Eve, who usurped Adam's authority, must learn to abide by her husband's headship, and Adam, because he squandered his sacrificial authority, must labor to exercise it nobly and retain it. To interpret the curse beset upon Eve as strictly a negative punitive consequence is to deny the goodness and fatherhood of God who wills that all men be saved.[221] Yes, God is a Father who forgives, yet punishes our offenses.[222]

---

221 See 1 Tm 2:4.
222 "Lord our God, you answered them; you were to Israel a forgiving God, though you punished their misdeeds." See Ps 99:8.

Though these conclusions may be difficult for modern man to accept, one cannot help but to acknowledge that often when a *pater familias* is robbed of his rightful authority of sacrificial responsibility the order of the family becomes subverted and souls are often misled and lost.

Many marriages endure the strife and tension that arises from woman undermining her husband's authority, or a man misusing or abdicating his own authority. Again, the key to saving marriages is not to abolish the man's rule, but that he understand, embrace, and live this rule properly.

Recall that the union of a man and woman and the offspring they bear was intended from the beginning to be a living reflection of the Triune God's self-giving love—an exchange of divine Persons. Yet, due to Adam's authority being subdued and subverted by Eve, his family did not achieve its end of revealing and reflecting the image and order of God's love.

In a similar way, if you, my brother, do not assume, exercise, and retain your office as head of the house and the duties of that office,[223] your family will fail to be a living reflection and human image of the Trinity's eternal exchange of love.

---

223 As outlined by Christ in Luke chapter 12: protect from thief; provide for family; be wise and prudent as the priest of the domestic church; all of which is at the service of God and the members of his household.

St. Joseph, Lord of His Household[224]

The *Roman Missal*'s opening antiphon for the Holy Mass on March 19th, the Solemnity of St. Joseph, Spouse of the Blessed Virgin Mary, reads:

> Behold, a faithful and prudent steward whom the
> Lord set over his household.[225]

This phrase, which hails the illustrious St. Joseph, is derived from the words our Lord Jesus uses to describe the *oikodespotes*, the head of the household, the *pater familias*.[226] This indicates that the Church sees a profound connection between St. Joseph, the man set "over the household" of the Holy Family, and the attributes of the *pater familias* as expressed by Christ: protector, provider, and, in a certain qualified sense, the minister of service—the priest of his family.

The concept of the father of the family being understood as a type of priest is not something avant-garde but rooted in the heritage of Catholic thought. St. Augustine, during one of his

---

224 Litany of St. Joseph: He made him the lord of his household, and prince over all his possessions.
225 *Roman Missal*, Opening Antiphon for the Solemnity of St. Joseph, Spouse of the Blessed Virgin Mary, March 19.
226 See Lk 12:24–32.

homilies, addressed the fathers in the congregation saying, "My fellow bishops, fulfill my office in your homes." The office to which Augustine was referring was that of a bishop. The Greek word for bishop, *episcopus*, literally means overseer. In other words, the bishop of the family, the human father, is to care for the flock of his family by being a priest of his domestic church.

Indeed, traditionally, the bishops of the Catholic Church have carried a crosier or staff. In the West, the crosier took the form of a shepherd's crook, which was curved at the top, allowing the sheep to be hooked. This is a metaphorical reference to the bishop's role as a shepherd to his "flock," which itself is a reference to Christ the Good Shepherd.

Recall that our Lord referred to the devil as the father of lies, who comes to kill, steal, and destroy. [227] Therefore, it is the role of the good shepherd to shield his sheep from this demonic predator.

The human father, like Christ, is to be a "good shepherd" who lays down his life for his sheep. Unfortunately, many fathers have been struck by the devil, and, because of this, their children and wives—the sheep—have been scattered.[228] Indeed, many fathers neglect to sacrifice themselves on behalf of their family and, by doing so, unwittingly sacrifice their children to

227 See Jn 10:10.
228 Reference to Mt 26:31; Zec 13:7.

235

the evil one. Our Lord Jesus draws a distinction between the shepherd and the hireling:

> The hireling, and he that is not the shepherd, whose own the sheep are not, seeth the wolf coming, and leaveth the sheep, and flieth: and the wolf catcheth, and scattereth the sheep: And the hireling flieth, because he is a hireling: and he hath no care for the sheep. (John 10:12–13)

Too often, my brother, we fathers succumb to the temptation to hire ourselves out for the advantages of the world and the appetites of the flesh, rather than laboring as the bishop who shepherds his flock by protecting, providing, and being the priest of the domestic church.

When a father submits to these temptations, he forgets that his family is the flock that God has placed under his care and that it is his responsibility to shepherd them lest they be scattered. A good shepherd, however, lays down his life of pride and envy in exchange for serving his family.

St. Joseph was granted the noble mission to be the shepherd of the Good Shepherd (Jesus Christ), the *pater familias* of his household, and the father to the Son of God the Father.

As mentioned previously, this authority is continually

confirmed by God, who, after the angelic Annunciation to the Blessed Virgin, communicated his directives for the Holy Family exclusively to St. Joseph.

Additionally, the twelve-year-old Jesus, who after being lost for three days was found by his parents, did not remain in "his Father's house,"[229] but rather "went down with them, and came to Nazareth, and was subject to them" (Lk 2:51).

Yet, St. Joseph did not assume his authority over his household presumptuously. Rather, animated by a holy fear and a conviction that he was not worthy of leading the holiest of all creatures, preeminent with grace, the Blessed Virgin Mary and the Son of God within her womb, "Joseph, being a just man and unwilling to put her to shame, resolved to send her away quietly."[230] Unlike Adam, St. Joseph refused to expose the Virgin to the potential sins of man. This humility is the foundational characteristic and prerequisite of the *pater familias,* who "is not come to be ministered unto, but to minister, and to give his life as redemption for many" (Mt 20:28)

This holy fear, combined with profound humility, is the hallmark of the true shepherd who will not resort to being a hireling who flees from the evil one, but rather, in times of adversity

---

229 See Lk 2:49.
230 *RC,* 3.

and persecution, does all in his power to unite his family in the love of God.

St. Joseph's fatherly office was at the service of the redemption of the family and mankind:

> Saint Joseph was called by God to serve the person and mission of Jesus directly *through the exercise of his fatherhood*. It is precisely in this way that, as the Church's Liturgy teaches, he "cooperated in the fullness of time in the great mystery of salvation" and is truly a "minister of salvation." His fatherhood is expressed concretely "in having made his life a service, a sacrifice to the mystery of the Incarnation and to the redemptive mission connected with it; in having used the legal authority, which was his over the Holy Family in order to make a total gift of self, of his life and work; in having tended his human vocation to domestic love into a superhuman oblation of self, an oblation of his heart and all his abilities into love placed at the service of the Messiah growing up in his home. (*Redemptoris Custos*, 8)

This being the case, it is in the Holy Family, the original "Church in miniature (*Ecclesia Domestica*)," that every Christian family must be reflected. "Through God's mysterious design, it was in that family that the Son of God spent long years of a hidden life. It is therefore the prototype and example of all Christian families. (*Redemptoris Custos*, 7)

If the Holy Family is the prototype and example of all Christian families, then we must conclude that St. Joseph's fatherhood is the paradigm and example—par excellence—for all fathers. St. Joseph, as "head of the household" became the least of his family by becoming a "supreme oblation" for the mystery of God.

My brother, let us imitate St. Joseph and exercise our charitable authority to serve the Creator by serving the creature. When we respond to God by being responsible for our families, we are not far from the Kingdom of God—for the divine Kingdom, the love of the Triune God, lives amidst our domestic church.

Jesus: The Lord of God's House

The Greek term *oikodespotes*, translated as master of the house, or householder, is a unique masculine noun exclusively used in Scripture by Jesus Christ himself on a dozen occasions. In several, if not most of these passages, the Lord Jesus refers to himself, through the use of parables, as the *oikodespotes*, the master of the house.[231] The fact that Jesus is the only person in the scriptures to use this word, and the fact that He exclusively applies the term to Himself, appears to indicate that our Lord is clearly stating that He is the ultimate *pater familias,* who shall "reign in the house of Jacob for ever" (Lk 1:33). He is the ruler of "his own house: which house we are" (Heb 3:6) and the "high priest over the house of God" (Heb 10:21).

As the typological fulfillment of all householders who preceded him, particularly the original Adam and St. Joseph, Christ establishes the ultimate example and paradigm of being the master of His house, mandating that all masters of their households follow his lead:

> The disciple is not above his master, nor the servant above his lord. It is enough for the disciple that he be as his master, and the servant of his lord. If they have called the goodman of the house [*oikodespotes*] Beelzebub, how much more them of his household? (Matthew 10:24–25)

---

231 See Mt 10:25; 13:27, 52; 20:1; 21:33; Lk 13:25; 14:21.

Our Lord sternly warns the *pater familias*, who rules in the image and succession of Christ, that he will be persecuted and identified as the enemy—even the devil himself—if he is faithful to his fatherly mission.

My brother, fatherhood and the divine mandate to rule over one's house will inevitably and consistently be misunderstood and maligned as being oppressive and tyrannical. The human father, the master of his house, is the sign of contradiction to an effeminate, radically feminized, egalitarian, conformist, and hedonistic society.

Yet, the *pater familias* is a great sign of hope. He stands as the unshakeable and unmovable sign of the restored family who reflects the Trinitarian image. Yes, he is a beacon of hope, a steady light that shines boldly amidst the darkness of this age, a luminous shaft that pierces the black cloud of sin, signaling that the devil cannot and will not prevail. Indeed, he is a living reflection of God the Father that shines in the darkness, and the darkness cannot overcome it.[232] A world that prefers the darkness of sin over the light of Christ will be convinced by the devil that the human father is a figure of Beelzebub.

---

232 See Jn 1.

The true *oikodespotes* will resist the temptation to compromise his faith for the flesh, the world, and the devil. As with Christ, his conviction to defend the garden at all cost will eventually claim his life—either by physical martyrdom, or death to his pride and selfishness. Nevertheless, he is summoned to battle, and the context for combat is the garden. On the night of Christ's betrayal, "Jesus came with [his disciples] into a country place which is called Gethsemani" (Mt 26:36).

In the cases of Adam and Jesus the New Adam, the garden is not only a literal place (as mentioned previously) but also a rich symbol of woman, the domestic life, the bride, and the Church, which is created to be man's delight as the word Eden indicates.[233] Yet, Christ, on the eve of his Passion and Death, entered the garden that was called Gethsemane, which is translated as "oil press."

As mentioned previously, by understanding the garden to be a rich symbol of woman and the domestic life, if not the Church herself, we begin to understand from these symbols and figures that man's responsibility for the garden, the woman, and even the Church in Christ's case is created by God to be a delight, but can often become the context of indescribable tension,

---

233 The Hebrew meaning of the word "Eden" is delight.

temptation, and agony. It is in the face of such intense trials that the master of the house will be tempted to flee from his post.

My brother, we must not gloss over this point. The householder's responsibility for the members of his house is of such tremendous import that the devil will continually assail him and batter him with severe temptations for the purpose of driving him from his vocational responsibility.

The garden becomes the crucible, the place of testing, and the very means to forge a man into a true sacrificial father who is capable of imaging Christ. In fact, the test is of such severe nature that even Jesus himself "fell upon his face, praying, and saying: My Father, if it be possible, let this chalice pass from me. Nevertheless, not as I will, but as Thou wilt" (Mt 26:39).

My brother, do not be scandalized by your personal resistance to self-donation and even the potentiality of martyrdom. The flesh, by its very nature, is opposed to the Spirit.[234] The flesh's natural response to sacrifice of self is resistance. Do not let the fear of self-sacrifice plunge you into despair. This fear is evidence that you comprehend the full weight of your vocational responsibility. Yet, let not such responsibility crush you, dissuade you, or influence you to abandon your post.

---

234 "For the flesh lusteth against the spirit: and the spirit against the flesh; for these are contrary one to another: so that you do not the things that you would." Gal 5:17.

We admire not those men who tell others that they have no fear, but rather we respect those who have striven to overcome fear and have been victorious in the face of fear. All men suffer, but few men sacrifice. We respect only those men who upon encountering or enduring a plight offer themselves and their suffering without complaint or boastfulness to God as a personal oblation.

The personal oblation born from the responsibility to provide and protect one's household is the priestly role of the domestic church's father. Indeed, we admire only those who sacrifice themselves, in spite of fear, for the sake of others.

Though Christ begged His father for the chalice of martyrdom to pass Him by, nevertheless, He entered the "oil press" of the garden, and, remaining steadfast, He resisted any urge to flee from His enemy and handed himself over for the sake of sacrificing Himself for His Bride, the future Church.

You and I will be tempted continually to flee the garden, to choose self-preservation at the expense of fulfilling God's will. Ironically, by preserving our lives, we will lose the vitality of a life fully lived. Indeed, "he that will save his life shall lose it: and he that shall lose his life for [Christ's] sake, shall find it" (Mt 16:25).

At the time of Jesus, the process of extracting oil from olives was called treading. Olives were set in a small cove or well of a rock and crushed by another rock, excreting the oil from the olive into the cove of the rock. This process occurred in Gethsemane (oil press)—hence the name.

When you, as the householder, press forward—like Christ, and like St. Joseph—to set the pace of self-giving love, you will often experience the burden and sting of rejection, resistance, and perhaps even betrayal from your wife and children, and most assuredly from the world. In a sense, the *pater familias* will be "tread." Yet, as you undergo the crushing blows to your pride and selfishness, if you embrace such suffering properly, the oil of charity, forgiveness, and forbearance, and the freedom to love without expecting anything in return, will be squeezed from you and anoint your wife and children. This is especially difficult to accept when a man's sacrificial love is not reciprocated. Again, St. John of the Cross assures us, "Where there is no love, put love, and there will be love."

Unfortunately, such pressure and conflict can compel us, much like Jesus' disciples on the night of His betrayal, to flee the garden. Often men will remain happily in the garden if it affords them the fruit of delight, but, if the garden becomes an oil press that begins to demand that more love be squeezed from them, they flee. What a man is and does under duress is what he truly is.

This process of treading is essential for you to become the *pater familias*, a man capable of glorifying God. Only by means of suffering can we attain our full capacity to love. "Suffering exists in order to unleash love in the human person."[235]

Suffering, particularly within marriage and the family, if embraced, can serve to unite the couple and the family, while also offering children an example of heroic, enduring, self-giving love. When this happens, the bitterness of Gethsemane can become truly what it should be, a garden of delight.

The garden, and man's responsibility for it, is indeed the "oil press" that metaphorically squeezes love from a man. This "oil" is the "oil of gladness"[236] that "anoints" his family with joy that stems from self-giving love. The householder's sacrifice unites the family and fosters deep and abiding unity. "Behold how good and how pleasant it is for brethren to dwell in unity," says the psalmist, "like the precious ointment on the head, that ran down upon the beard, the beard of Aaron, Which ran down to the skirt of his garment (Ps 132:2). Aaron, as priest chosen by God, was anointed with oil. In a similar, mystically spiritual way, you, as priest of your domestic church, are anointed by

---

235 John Paul II, *Salvifici Doloris*, 8.
236 A reference to Ps 45:7.

God with oil, the imparting of His Spirit,[237] which is no cowardly Spirit, and it is this oil of gladness that is the key to the unification of your family.

False Seeds Sown

"Responsibility is man's ability to respond to God."[238] Yet, one can only respond to His commander if he has received his command. It is imperative that the *pater familias*, if he is to be a sign of contradiction to this age of darkness, listens attentively for the voice of God that is primarily received by embracing and fulfilling his vocation. Indeed, the word vocation is derived from the Latin word *vox*, which means voice. Therefore, to receive the *vox* of God, it is imperative "that you walk worthy of the vocation in which you are called" (Eph 4:1).

Your vocation as father and head of your household, the father of the family, is your path to holiness and sanctification. How many men are no longer capable of "hearing" the *vox* of God? By rejecting or neglecting their vocation of fatherhood, they have rejected the very means and ability to discern God's directive and will for their lives.

---

237 "For God hath not given us the spirit of fear: but of power, and of love, and of sobriety." 2 Tm 1:7.

238 Peter Kreeft, *Back to Virtue*; San Francisco, CA, Ignatius Press, 1986.

If the captain of a ship is misguided, so also the ship and its crew will be lost. How many families are lost, if not drowning, in the black sea of the flesh, the world, and slavery to the devil because fathers have neglected to remain steadfast in the vocation they have been called to?

The devil stands poised and ready for combat with the purpose of drawing you from your vocational path. He is bent on deposing the *pater familias* in order that he may rule in his place, substituting self-donation with slavery to sin.

The evil one is acutely aware that God has summoned you to be an icon of God the Father, a manifestation of God's fatherly glory, and therefore he will stop short of nothing to drive and derail you from your fatherly vocation.

The evil one's strategy can be described as having four aspects or stages: temptation (always rooted in some type of deception, a false suggestion to the imagination), intimidation, distraction, and isolation.

The essence of this truth is outlined by our Lord in the parable of the Sower and the Seed.[239] Our Lord interprets the birds that steal the seed sowed on the wayside as the devil who robs man of the seed of the Word, the *vox* of God, which

---

239 See Mt 13:1–23.

directs us to the accomplishment of God's will by means of our fatherly vocation.

The devil is intent, by means of temptation, on stealing the seed of God's Word before it can take root. When the *pater familias* is bound by such temptations, he becomes deaf to the divine Word and incapable of transmitting this Word and its wisdom to his wife and children. Thus, his leadership becomes ineffective, if not supplanted by the devil.

If the devil cannot compel the head of the house into temptation, he will most certainly use intimidation to drive him from his vocational path.

Our Lord Jesus described the seed that fell on rocky soil and was scorched by the sun—due to its shallow roots—as a symbol of those men who initially believe, but, when faced with persecution or suffering because of their belief in Jesus Christ and their upholding of their vocational fatherly mission, lose heart and fall away.

If the tactics of temptation and intimidation are not effective in deterring the *pater familias* from fulfilling his vocation, the devil will use the art of distraction.

Our Lord described the seed that began to spring up but was choked by thorns and thistles as symbolizing the pursuit of pleasures, riches, and cares of the world. The evil one often will offer man something that has the appearance of good for the purpose of keeping him from that which is greatest—God and leading his family to Him.

The pursuit of riches, the incessant desire for comfort, the multiplication of hobbies and possessions, and the perpetual inclination toward pleasure, power, and prestige all have an element of goodness that the devil manipulates and uses to rob our attention from service and adoration of God, and of leading and serving the family.

If his tactics of temptation, intimidation, or distraction do not depose the father of the house, he will attempt to ensnare the household in isolation. Isolation is the consequence of separating ourselves from people because we are convinced that they are not worthy of us or our attention. By separating ourselves from serving our family, we separate ourselves from our God and Lord, "who did not come to be served, but to serve."[240] Originally, the Pharisees separated themselves from the world so as to be united wholly to God. Eventually, this sincere purpose became corrupted. Hence, the name Pharisee means "separated one."

There are grave consequences for the father who separates himself from service to his family: "Unless a grain of wheat

---

240 "For the Son of man also is not come to be ministered unto, but to minister, and to give his life a redemption for many." Mk 10:45.

falling into the ground die, itself remaineth alone" (Jn 12:24–25). My brother, if you isolate yourself from your family, neglecting your service to them, you will eventually be isolated, resented, and forgotten. This, in fact, is Hell. Yet, if you, the grain of wheat, fall to the ground and die to yourself in your domestic garden, you will bear much fruit—fruit that will endure.

A Summons to Stewardship

Though our Lord Jesus is the ultimate ruler of the house of God, His Church, He does not reserve this authority to himself exclusively, but allows His disciples to participate in this office.

St. Peter, in response to Christ's parable regarding the *pater familias,* asked, "Lord, dost thou speak this parable to us, or likewise to all?" (Lk 12:41), to which Lord responded:

> Who (thinkest thou) is the faithful and wise steward, whom his lord setteth over his family, to give them their measure of wheat in due season? . . . Verily I say to you, he will set him over all that he possesseth. (Luke 12:42, 44)

Though the steward can be interpreted universally as any father who is called by God to rule his house, Christ's words appear to appeal particularly to St. Peter and his successors.

Jesus, prior to making His route to Jerusalem to embrace the fate of His Passion and Death, journeyed with His disciples to Caesarea Philippi, where He asked them, "Whom do men say that the Son of man is?" (Mt 16:13). After their responses, Jesus asked, "But who do you say that I am?" (Mt 16:15), to which Simon Peter responded, "Thou art Christ, the Son of the living God" (Mt 16:16). Jesus then said to Peter:

> Blessed art thou, Simon Bar-Jona: because flesh and blood hath not revealed it to thee, but my Father who is in heaven. And I say to thee: That thou art Peter; and upon this rock I will build my church, and the gates of hell shall not prevail against it. And I will give to thee the keys of the kingdom of heaven. And whatsoever thou shalt bind upon earth, it shall be bound also in heaven: and whatsoever thou shalt loose upon earth, it shall be loosed also in heaven. (Matthew 16:17–19)

Our Lord, as ruler of the house, with full knowledge that his departure from this world was eminent, granted St. Peter the stewardship of His house, the Church, to be the vicar, an image of himself, the ultimate *pater familias*. It is St. Peter and his successors, who by their prudent and faithful leadership, give the members of the household, the Church, "bread," that is the Eucharist, and the Gospel in due season.

Our Lord's words addressed to St. Peter echo the words of God spoken by Isaiah the prophet to the steward of David's house, the ʿal- hab-bā-yiṯ, (over the household), Shebna, who had abused his office. By examining the scriptural passage that our Lord echoed, we will derive a vivid picture of the characteristics of the steward of the Lord's house.

> Thus saith the Lord God of hosts: Go, get thee in to him that dwelleth in the tabernacles, to Sobna who is over the temple: and do thou say to him . . . And I will drive thee out of thy station, and depose thee from thy ministry. And it shall come to pass in that day, that I will call my servant Eliacim the Son of Helcias, And I will clothe him with thy robe, and will strengthen him with thy girdle, and will give thy power into his hand: and he shall be a father to the inhabitants of Jerusalem, and the house of Juda. And I will lay the key of the house of David upon his shoulder: and he shall open, and none shall shut: and he shall shut, and none shall open. And I will

THE MEANING AND MYSTERY OF MAN

fasten him as a peg in a sure place, and he shall be
for a throne of glory to the house of his father. (Isaiah
22:15, 19–23)

Notice that Shebna has authority over the household of God,
second only to the king, the descendant of David, in whose
absence he reigned. Shebna's office of steward is a ministry as
vicar of the king and is transferable to another man as indicated
by the word "station," and also indicated by him being replaced
by Eliachim.

Associated with this office of stewardship comes power and
paternal authority. He shall be a "father to the inhabitants"
and have the authority to "open and shut," bind and loose, as
symbolized by the keys of the house of David.

Our Lord intentionally echoes God's words to Isaiah to
demonstrate that He, as the ruler of the House of God, the
Church, appointed a steward, a vicar, who would be second to
his Kingship—St. Peter and his successors.

This office characterized by power and paternal authority to
bind and to loose is symbolized by the keys to the Kingdom
of Heaven, which our Lord gives to St. Peter. For this reason,
we rightly refer to St. Peter, and his successors, as Pope, which
translated means papa, or father. Indeed, the steward of the

house of God, the Pope, is called to be a father to the family, the household of God.

It has come to pass, in these latter days of the Kingdom of God, that many of those who are called to the ordained office of ministry over the Lord's house in the station of bishop and priest, who are called to be *pater familias* in the image of Christ, have said in their hearts, "My lord is long in coming; and [have begun] to strike the menservants and maid servants, and to eat and drink and be drunk" (Lk 12:45).

Far too many of those entrusted with God's house have scandalized the members of His household, striking the servants with abuse and using the position of fatherly authority to serve themselves.

Our Lord has clearly and sternly expressed what the recompense will be for such men, "The lord of that servant will come in that day that he hopeth not, and at the hour that he knoweth not, and shall separate him, and shall appoint him his portion with unbelievers" (Lk 12:46).

It is to these shepherds that our Lord, as ruler of the house, has imparted his authority to be fathers of the family of God. Yet, many of fathers have fallen, compromising the faith in pursuit of "peace" between religions. They have succumbed to worldliness, prosperity, and comfort in the hopes of making

Christ's poverty and sacrifice more attractive. They have embraced inclusiveness for fear that the sword of truth should cut
at error and exclude those who reject it. And they have exalted
femininity at the demise and loss of masculinity and fatherhood. Effeminate, they cringe at the difficult teachings of Christ
and His Gospel and avoid these "contentious" passages as one
avoids a plague.

Omitting the complete version of these "contentious" read-
ings, they veil the human father's authority over his family, and
conceal the very Word of God that speaks of male headship that
will—in Christ's headship—save the family.[241]

Their neglect to be fathers spiritually and aid men in becoming spiritual fathers is a denial and rejection of the Father in
Heaven, whose image and love they ought to reflect. Theirs is
a sin of omission. The silence of Adam. It is for lack of vision
that God's people perish.[242] Indeed, it is these who neglect to
give men the true theological, scriptural vision of fatherhood.

241 According to the instructions of the *Lectionary*, the New Testament reading
from Colossians on the Solemnity of the Holy Family is offered in a shorter
form that omits the structure of the Christian family: "Wives, be subject to your
husbands, as it behoveth in the Lord. Husbands, love your wives and be not
bitter towards them. Children, obey your parents in all things: for this is well
pleasing to the Lord. Fathers, provoke not your children to indignation, lest they
be discouraged" (Col 3:18-21). This is obviously not due to the length of this
reading, considering its brevity.

242 See Prv 29:15.

Priests who neglect being spiritual fathers create an absence of fathers. By neglecting their own fatherhood, they have neglected in leading fathers, and, because of this neglect, the household of God endures a famine of fatherhood.

If there is none to lead, then none will follow; if fathers do not lead their families from evil, then evil will lead the family; and if a priestly father teaches not men to be father-priests, then the family of God will be fatherless and know not the heavenly Father.[243]

The blows of the Lord's wrath fall most heavily upon those who have been given the most responsibility:[244] "But woe to you . . . because you shut the kingdom of heaven against men, for you yourselves do not enter in; and those that are going in, you suffer not to enter" (Mt 23:13).

And again:

> Woe to the shepherds . . . that fed themselves: should not the flocks be fed by the shepherds? . . . And my sheep were scattered, because there was no shepherd: and they became the prey of all the beasts of the field, and were scattered . . . behold I myself come upon the shepherds, I will require my flock at their

---

243 See Mal 4:5–6.
244 See Lk 12:48.

hand, and I will cause them to cease from feeding the flock any more, neither shall the shepherd feed themselves anymore: and I will deliver my flock from their mouth, and it shall no more be meat for them . . . behold I myself will seek my sheep, and will visit them. (Ezekiel 34:2, 5, 10–11)

Both the priestly father and the human father are endowed with the tremendous responsibility to follow Christ and enter the garden. Rather than repeating the silence of Adam, who allowed the serpent to penetrate the garden of Eve, the true father, by means of his own self-oblation, anoints his flock with the oil of gladness, unifying the members of his household and uniting them to the ultimate Ruler of the House, Jesus Christ. This is his vocation. This is his glory. This is the meaning and mystery of man.

WHAT IF I DON'T HAVE A PLAN FOR MY LIFE?

WE CAN HELP.

KNOW YOUR **PURPOSE.**
BUILD YOUR **PLAN.**
UNLOCK THE **POWER.**

The Fathers of St. Joseph has developed a plan that helps men know their noble purpose and unlock God's power in their lives. Access the tools to help you become who God intended you to be—like St. Joseph, a father on earth like the Father in Heaven at:

FATHERSOFSTJOSEPH.ORG

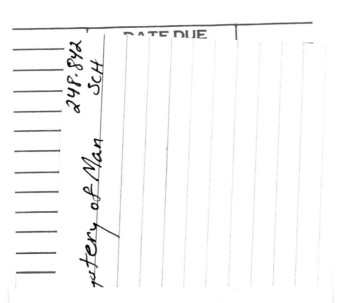

DATE DUE

248.842
SCH

...tery of Man

St. Stephen the Martyr Catholic
Church
13055 SE 192nd St,
Renton, WA 98058